Philip

The Gospel Ministry of  ist:
Scattered, Sent and Se

People IN THE BIBLE

William Wade

DayOne

Army Scripture Reader William Wade has written a truly remarkable and challenging book about Philip the Evangelist. Perhaps best known for his desert-highway encounter with the Ethiopian eunuch as recorded in Acts 8, Philip was an extraordinarily effective evangelist and ambassador for the exciting new movement begun by Jesus of Nazareth and followed by millions around the world today. The Christian gospel was only heard two thousand years ago because the early followers of Christ were scattered far and wide due to their persecution in Jerusalem. They had the conviction to preach the good news of Jesus wherever they were sent because of their faith in him and their motivating love for him. But this book focuses on Philip—an evangelist with an unusual background. His preparation came through looking after the early church's widows and after that crucible experience he was ready to be sent wherever God wanted him to preach the gospel. After many spiritual adventures he settled in Caesarea and consolidated a young church that would stand firmly in the face of its critics. William Wade's description of the evangelistic work of Philip in his day is a call to arms to us in our day, to take as a serious challenge the commission to 'Go into all the world and preach the gospel to every creature' (Mark 16:15). William Wade's book challenges our commitment to that commission.

Lord Dannatt GCB CBE MC

Over fifteen years ago a precious young man came to my home and asked me to pray with him. He told me his name was William Wade and he was embarking on a journey both physical and spiritual. He was to become an evangelist to the British Forces in Germany and he is now working for Christ in England. It was a privilege to pray with him and for him as I have since witnessed his progress in God among many young men, sharing their problems and difficulties. But what also impresses me is his knowledge of the things of God. Reading this book I said to myself, 'Here is a man who understands the gospel and knows what he is talking about.'

I heartily recommend this book to any young preacher who wants to be a servant of God. Read it, and let William Wade, under God, become a blessing to you.

May God bless this book to the person who has a heart to win souls, and may God continue to use William Wade.

Dr James McConnell, Metropolitan Tabernacle, Belfast

William Wade has worked very hard to think through the pen portraits we have of Philip the Evangelist in the New Testament. Thankfully, he's worked equally hard to apply them to the contemporary church. It's wonderful, therefore, to have a book which brings Philip's life and example out of the shadows. I kept finding my heart beating faster.

Rico Tice, All Souls Church, London, and co-author of Christianity Explored

© Day One Publications 2016

ISBN 978-1-84625-541-0

Unless otherwise indicated, Scripture quotations are from the **New King James Version (NKJV)®**. Copyright © 1982 by Thomas Nelson, Inc. Used by permission. All rights reserved.

British Library Cataloguing in Publication Data available

Published by Day One Publications
Ryelands Road, Leominster, HR6 8NZ
Telephone 01568 613 740 FAX 01568 611 473
email—sales@dayone.co.uk
web site—www.dayone.co.uk

North America—email—usasales@dayone.co.uk

All rights reserved
No part of this publication may be reproduced, or stored in a retrieval system, or transmitted, in any form or by any means, mechanical, electronic, photocopying, recording or otherwise, without the prior permission of Day One Publications.

Cover design by Rob Jones, Elk Design
Printed by TJ International

This book is dedicated to five men who have had gospel impact on my life:

Pastor Tommy Latimer, who first preached the gospel to me;

Pastor Roy Kerr, who gave me opportunities to explore gospel preaching;

Pastor Paul Reid, who continues to manage the tension of gospel preaching in the twenty-first century;

Pastor Jack McKee, who is still preaching the gospel in the most difficult area of the UK after over thirty years;

Pastor James McConnell, who has left a legacy of fearless gospel preaching to succeeding generations.

Contents

INTRODUCTION	8
1 BACKGROUND AND CONTEXT: PHILIP THE MAN (ACTS 6–7)	10
2 THE SCATTERING AND THE SENDING: GOD'S ROLE (AND OURS) IN MISSION (ACTS 8:1, 4)	21
3 PHILIP THE EVANGELIST: HIS MESSAGE AND MINISTRY (ACTS 8:5–8)	31
4 THE SPIRITUAL INTERFACE: CONFRONTATION ON THE DEVIL'S DOORSTEP (ACTS 8:6–24)	42
5 ESTABLISHING THE DISCIPLES: MULTI-GIFT MINISTRY (ACTS 8:14–17)	51
6 FROM THE SPOTLIGHT TO THE SHADOWS: RADICAL OBEDIENCE TO RADICAL GUIDANCE (ACTS 8:26–40)	59
7 ITINERANT AND STATIC: PHILIP'S EVANGELISTIC MINISTRY AS MODEL (ACTS 8:40)	65
CONCLUSION	72

Introduction

Evangelism. What emotion do you feel when you read that word? Excitement? Exhilaration? Caution? Fear? Uncertainty? What picture is conjured up in your mind? Placards? Preaching? Conversation? Suits? Stadiums? 'Evangelism' is a word that usually gets a reaction, be it positive, negative or indifferent. Whatever your reaction is, this book chronicles that of a first-century disciple who found himself thrown into the most adventurous, unpredictable, and at times downright strange contexts as the early church found itself rapidly changing under the weight of both blessing and persecution. In the reactions of this one man we find insights, hints and a clear blueprint of what gospel ministry could and, it might be argued, should look like in our apparently postmodern twenty-first-century Western world.

I remember the first time my heart fluttered in response to the topic of evangelism. I had not long committed my life to Jesus Christ and was attending a prayer meeting in the living room of one of the members of our little pioneer church. While some were just settling in for the evening, and others were in the kitchen having their tea poured and adding a biscuit or two to the accompanying saucer, our host mentioned that he had a video tape of a meeting in America. He promptly pushed it into the video player and pressed 'play'. Some people were still milling around between the living room and kitchen, some were still coming in from the street, and others were just having a general chat. I, however, was quickly transfixed by the television screen. What I saw was an American evangelist preach so dramatically that I could not take my eyes off him. The setting was a sports stadium and it was full to capacity. There was emotional singing, lights, people weeping in the audience. To a young man who was also a very young Christian, it was instantly alluring. From that moment on, I believed that that setting and those scenes were what real evangelism looked like and how a real evangelist should be measured. Surely, if God could do it there, he could do it here, I thought. That measuring stick of how evangelism should look permeated the UK in what became known as 'the Billy Graham effect': the lone, suited evangelist preaching with an open Bible in his hand in a propositional, anecdotal style to a crowd, be it large or small.

This may not be the case today, as the psyche of the Western church has shifted from that image of evangelism to styles which revolve around the Alpha Course, or even to planting gardens in deprived areas or facilitating free hugs in the street. Evangelism has morphed as society has morphed. Some of those new styles have simply reflected contextual variations while maintaining a clear biblically based gospel message; the Christianity Explored course is an example. Others, however, not only have become slaves to context, but also have shaped the gospel message itself to fit in with an increasingly subjective society. Still others have sought to remove the gospel *message* in preference to a *mission* which suggests that social action leads to the redemption of a human soul. Evangelism, it seems, can mean all things to all people.

This book tells the story of one man who pioneered evangelism. This book also exposes and often challenges what is evidenced in contemporary culture under the banner of evangelistic ministry. If you are involved in gospel work, are intrigued by the role of the evangelist, have a theological desire to understand the beginnings of church mission or have a wider interest in the New Testament church, then I pray that, as you read this book, you will be gripped by the Word of God under the power of his Holy Spirit, and will be re-ignited by a passion to be an active witness in the world at this crucial hour.

Chapter 1

Background and context: Philip the man (Acts 6–7)

It must have been a harrowing, if somewhat surreal, experience to have stood and watched as Jesus the Christ ascended physically into heaven (Acts 1). As soon as he had disappeared out of sight, those early disciples must have begun to reflect on how their lives had unfolded over the previous three and a half years. They had been on a roller-coaster ride of faith with an itinerant preacher from Nazareth who had made it increasingly clear that he was more than just a religious zealot or even a compassionate teacher. This was the promised Messiah: the glory of Israel and the Son of the living God! It must have been life-changing to have been part of that little travelling band of ministers-in-training!

And yet how isolated they must have felt as their Lord and Master returned to his Father. They had received the promise that Jesus would be with them always, even until the end of the age (Matt. 28:18)—a promise which rests on the church until the time of his return. However, they also faced the reality of growing antagonism from their extremely fervent religio-political culture. On the one hand, the Jewish leaders in Jerusalem were forcefully opposing anyone who was identified with Jesus of Nazareth; and on the other, the Roman authorities were vehemently opposed to anyone who said that there was any Lord other than Caesar. The disciples, now simply living on a promise, returned to the heart of Jerusalem with enemies seemingly all around them. But this turned out to be the perfect scenario for God to work!

As promised, the Holy Spirit came with power on the day of Pentecost as a mighty rushing wind (Acts 2:2). The church was born in Jerusalem, and the disciples would never be the same again. Peter famously stood up and proclaimed the bold but good news that the same Jesus who had been crucified just weeks before had risen and was now seated at the right hand of God in heaven. As a response to the pleas of the crowd regarding their standing before God, Peter went on to challenge them to repent and be baptized for the remission of their sins, and at least three thousand responded (2:14–41). The church of Jesus Christ was born with revival power! After the Pentecost initiation, the believers grew in number and strength, with open witness in Solomon's porch, in the temple and from house to house. Miracles, arrests, building-shaking prayer and divine judgements followed the early consolidation of the church in Jerusalem.

At this stage we can make two important observations: first; the church was born with explosive power; and second, the church grew with increasing boldness. These two observations are crucial to understanding the mindset and ministry of an evangelist who would soon be thrust out of Jerusalem and into an unevangelized city called Samaria.

It is vital to see that the normal Christian experience of those early days of the church was marked by power and boldness, two hallmarks which are sadly lacking in much of contemporary Christianity. It has been astutely observed that the early church had power, whereas the contemporary church has PowerPoint. As we turn to look at this man called Philip, we need to understand that Philip was born again into this kind of Christian experience. He had obviously responded to the call to repent and be baptized, for that was the teaching of the church, under Peter and the other apostles, on how to become a part of the church. It was not through family ties, attendance at meetings or by birth. Those man-made regulations would come around three centuries later under the reign of Emperor Constantine. No, the only way to be admitted into this new body of Jesus-followers, known as 'the Way', was to repent and be baptized for the remission of sins. Not only had Philip done this at some stage (on the day of Pentecost, perhaps?), but by the time we are

Chapter 1

introduced to him in Acts 6 he had become an embedded member of this new-found band of believers.

It should be of little surprise that with the rush of new converts into this newly formed body of believers came one or two teething problems. The first serious issue presented itself over the care of widows, although the heart of the matter could be found at a deeper level in the identity of Greeks and Hebrews. It seems that the Hebrew widows were being ministered to materially in a way which placed the Greek widows of the church at a disadvantage (Acts 6:1). The response from the apostles was that, rather than them being sidetracked from their priority mission, the believers should appoint seven other godly men to serve in this matter. The outcome was that Stephen, Philip, Prochorus, Nicanor, Timon, Parmenas and Nicolas were chosen, as they were full of the Holy Spirit and wisdom and had a good reputation among the others.

Very rarely do any of God's significantly used servants waltz straight into a ready-made pulpit or into a patiently waiting revival. Normally, there is a waiting time in which not only are they developed as useful servants of God, but they are also tested, in order that they might develop a character which is commensurate with the calling. We see this principle vividly in the life of Joseph (see Gen. 37–50). He had been given a clear calling to leadership in the form of two very specific dreams. You would think that, from then on, it would simply be a matter of him walking into his God-given destiny. Not so; there was first a severe period of testing to develop Joseph for national leadership. He had to endure being sold as a common slave, being forsaken by his family, being falsely accused of sexual immorality and being falsely imprisoned. Yet it was while he was in prison that God began to root out any trace of pride, ambition and self-seeking, in order that Pharaoh might be able to say of Joseph, 'Can we find such a one as this, a man in whom is the Spirit of God?' (Gen. 41:38). Not only did Joseph find release, promotion and national leadership resulting from his interpretation of Pharaoh's dreams, but his time of character development allowed him both to give God the glory throughout the whole process and to maintain the calling placed on his life with dignity, integrity and wisdom.

We see this pattern played out even in the life of Jesus. John publicly affirmed that Jesus of Nazareth was the Lamb of God sent to take away the sin of the world (John 1:29), and he then baptized him. As Jesus was coming up out of the water, his Father spoke from heaven to say that this was his own beloved Son, 'in whom I am well pleased' (Matt. 3:17). A Hollywood movie script would have taken Jesus straight from there into a dynamic miracle-working ministry. However, the very next verse in Matthew (4:1) tells us that God's Spirit led Jesus into the wilderness to be tempted by the devil. The pattern of calling, followed by adversity, followed by commission, is seen in Jesus' life, for, after the forty days of temptation in the desert, Jesus returned victorious and then marched into the drama of a three-and-a-half-year earthly ministry which was unlike anything the world had ever seen.

We can also trace this pattern of calling, adversity and commission in the lives of Moses, David, Daniel, Peter and Paul. Let us not think that the calling which God places on our lives will be issued one day and carried out in all its glory the next; God allows the valleys to be placed on our journey so that we can handle the heights of the mountains he calls us to climb.

Philip clearly had a calling on his life, for when the church in Jerusalem needed to choose seven men who were full of the Holy Spirit, full of wisdom and with a good report among them all, his name was offered. Yet instead of God giving Philip a dream or vision to go from Jerusalem to Samaria in order to begin some evangelistic work, Philip was expected to serve locally to solve the dispute concerning widows and to ease their grievances. This is hardly the stuff of the Christian superstar. There was no cry from Philip claiming that he was better than this; that his calling trumped this menial task; that he was destined for city-wide revival

Chapter 1

campaigns. Scripture tells us that he simply got on with it. He was neither a prima donna nor a drama queen about his task concerning the church widows. He just served.

Not only did Philip's service at this level bless the widows, but also it had a ripple effect on the Jerusalem church on a wider scale. His service at this level allowed the apostles to concentrate on the Word and prayer, and on their mission of spreading the faith and establishing the growing church. His service displayed a measure of humility and servanthood to the wider church body, and it also prepared him to be used in a greater manner once his commissioning time did come; he would have experience of the baggage that new converts can bring into the church. Serving time, much like preparation time, is never wasted in the greater economy of God's timetable.

Unfortunately, a different pattern has developed within much of the Western church, and it runs something like this. A person, possibly young, in the local church senses a calling to ministry. This is followed by a period of excitement, during which time the person is usually advised to decide which Bible college to attend. The person is then sent away to Bible college for around three years, gains an academic qualification, and is usually automatically ushered into a small church in order to begin 'the ministry'. Going from conceptual idea to running a church can sometimes take as little as three years, and I've seen it happen in far less time.

A disclaimer before I continue: I am not against Bible colleges. I attended one and gained a lot of wisdom out of the experience. But Bible college should not be the priority training ground for any potential minister; the local church should be. This can, of course, be problematic if pastors of local churches are either theologically inept or insensitive leaders. If that is the case, the need is to find a more theologically robust and spiritually sensitive pastor. Scripture is clear about the training of up-and-coming ministers: they should be trained in the local church by wise leaders (think of the relationship between Paul and Timothy). Also, there seems to be a very quick turnaround between the initial sense of calling and the shipping-off to Bible college. What about slowing down a little? I realize that this is difficult, especially with young people who are keen to be leading world revivals and establishing the biggest church in the nation—but let us remember the inherent power of service on a smaller scale. If we allowed more of our young people to serve in the local church for a significant period of time before being hurtled off to Bible college, we might not have so many aloof, management–executive-type leaders in local churches today; we might have more shepherds of the flock.

Philip learned to serve in the local church and he did it under the power of the Holy Spirit. The real spiritual work was not only being carried out by the apostles as miracles were taking place; it takes a work of the Holy Spirit to serve God well in any capacity in the church or in the world. As Philip was helping to serve the widows, Stephen, no doubt a friend of Philip's and certainly a fellow-labourer in the church, began to be used much as the apostles were: in miracles and 'signs among the people' (Acts 6:8). Of course, the beginnings of persecution had already come with Peter and John's arrests in Acts 4, and, now that Stephen was being so greatly used of God, a hornets' nest was stirred up and he was reported by antagonistic zealots to the religious council of Jerusalem, charged with blasphemy—a crime he did not commit.

Stephen's service to God and to the church turned out to be more of a sprint than a marathon. With his face like that of an angel (Acts 6:15), Stephen defended his new-found faith in Jesus the Christ before the high priest of the council in a dramatic speech which covered the call of Abraham, the life of Joseph, the deliverance of Israel under Moses, the rebellion of Israel, the kingship of David, and the charge that Israel had become stiff-necked and had resisted the word of the prophets by murdering Jesus of Nazareth. It was a stunning rebuke to the religious authorities, who had also been charged by Jesus with being proud,

Chapter 1

haughty and hypocritical (Matt. 23:1–36). Now they were receiving more of the same from one of Jesus' followers.

What a stirring example of boldness Stephen is here! Not only did he defend his belief in the identity and innocence of Jesus the Christ, but also he challenged the religious hypocrisy of the ruling council of Jerusalem in their refusal to acknowledge that they had murdered the very Son of God. How the Western church could do with more of the likes of this man! As I write, there is an ongoing court case in Northern Ireland over a bakery run by Christians who have refused to make a cake with an iced topping brandishing words in support of gay marriage. The UK (and even some news feeds in North America) has gone wild with the story, unleashing a tsunami of criticism over the stance which the bakery owners have chosen to take. Thankfully, the Christian Institute has taken on the case and has unswervingly stood for the liberty of this bakery to make a decision on spiritual grounds. The owners are walking in the shadows of Stephen the martyr. But we need more Stephens in our lands today. Where are the Stephens challenging the ignorance of Western governments concerning the beheading of Christians in the Middle East? Where are the Stephens standing on our streets proclaiming the good news of Jesus Christ in a post-secular age? Where are the Stephens walking into the no-go Muslim areas of the Western world and challenging that blinded community with the claims of the gospel? Please, God, raise up more like Stephen in these last of the last days!

Unsurprisingly, the council were cut to the heart and even more so when Stephen looked up and proclaimed that he saw Jesus standing at the right hand of the Father in heaven (Acts 7:56). They could take no more. They cast him out of the city and stoned him. They could not handle the itinerant preacher from Nazareth who had had such a large following for over three years, and now they could not handle one of his followers accusing them in much the same way he had done. So they replicated the sentence: death. However, Martin Luther King stated that

Background and context

you cannot kill an idea, and neither can you kill a belief just by killing one or two people who hold to it. The council would shortly understand that principle. Stephen died defending his Lord; he died serving in the church; he died having been used of God in miracles and wonders among the people; he died as the proto-martyr of the church. No, Stephen did not establish churches all over the known world as Paul eventually did, and he did not have a long life of unending service in the local church—but while he lived, he made his life count for his Saviour. He did what he could, while he could. He is a great example of working 'while it is day', for sometimes the night comes suddenly, when we least expect it, and then we can do no more work. Let us live like Stephen in his boldness, service, humility and attitude—an attitude that says, 'While I have breath and another day to live, I will serve Jesus Christ with everything I have!'

As Acts 7 draws to a tragic—and yet for Stephen, glorious—close, the final words that Stephen utters lead us to the dark figure of a man possessed by the desire to see the church of Jesus Christ wiped utterly off the face of the earth: Saul of Tarsus. Those last words of Stephen called for the forgiveness of those who were stoning him—murdering him; and standing watching and nodding his head in approval was this man Saul. Books upon books would later be written about him, but what of our main character, Philip? What are we to make of him at this stage in his journey towards a dynamic and long-lasting evangelistic ministry that spanned decades? We can already begin to see a number of factors shaping Philip's life as a believer and his preparation for being used in city-wide revival.

First, Philip's expectation of normal Christian experience was church growth. The church in Jerusalem had been born out of a staggering response of thousands to Peter's brave and Spirit-inspired speech on the day of Pentecost. Following this first explosion of converts, the church continued to grow as the Word of God spread throughout the city, even in the midst of the beginnings of persecution. Second, Philip's experience of

Chapter 1

service as a minister to the disputing widows provided him with an ethic of involvement. In other words, in service to God he was ready to respond to need wherever a need presented itself. He was 'wired to serve'. Third, Philip saw an example of apostolic ministry which helped him form his own view of what valid Christian ministry should look like. He saw boldness in the face of persecution and criticism; prayer when faced with challenge (Acts 4:23–31); the clear preaching of Jesus as the Christ of God, able to save the human soul from sin; power accompanying the preaching of Scripture as a demonstration of the presence of God's Holy Spirit; the experience of the infilling of the Holy Spirit as divine energy for Christian life and service; and the focus on seeing the lost converted to follow Jesus as Lord and to become part of 'the Way'—the church of God.

Each of these shaping factors helps us to understand the man who would shortly find himself in a backslidden city called Samaria, and to see why he began to live out a ministry which impacted the whole city with the joy of the Lord. What are the factors shaping our lives, and how might they enable us to fulfil a work for God where we are placed?

It has been said that the way a person becomes a Christian, and the kind of church environment that person becomes integrated into, are life-shaping for the rest of that Christian's experience. I was first challenged directly by the gospel message when two fifteen-year-old girls gatecrashed a party I was having one Saturday night on the edge of Belfast. The two girls came from a local church plant and decided to make an evangelistic foray into our drunken assembly. They turned the music off, stood in the centre of the living room and told us that God loved us, that Jesus Christ his Son had died for the forgiveness of our sin, and that we needed to get right with God—to be 'saved', 'born again'. It was bizarre. They challenged us to go to church with them the next evening, and we said 'yes', just to get rid of them. As it turned out, a group of us bumped into these two young girls the next night and they urged us to go to their gospel service. We tried to say 'no', but they persisted, until finally a member of our little group suggested we go along to disrupt the meeting. And so we went, sat in the back row of the corrugated-iron community hall and made a mockery of all that was going on.

However, as soon as the preacher stood up to preach, we suddenly became still and we listened to his every word. He spoke with authority, passion, directness and what seemed at the time to be truth. We found out later that it was indeed truth, as he preached on the identity of Jesus as the Son of God; of his mission to die on the cross for our sin; of the eternal destinies of heaven and hell; of the power of God not only to save a soul, but also to keep it. To cut a long and dramatic story short, three weeks later, four of us committed our young lives to following Jesus Christ. Over those first few weeks, this pastor had us testifying to the saving power of God to all our friends and to the housing estate in general at the church's weekly open-air services. It was a nerve-shattering experience, but it was also a wonderful experience—and a wise one too, with regard to that pastor's desire to see us established in our blossoming faith. That is how I came into the Christian faith. Perhaps, then, it is little surprise that I am now an evangelist with SASRA (Soldiers and Airmen's Scripture Readers Association[1]) to the British Forces. I often go into the barrack blocks and the soldiers' rooms to speak of Jesus—much as those two fifteen-year-old girls did with me and my friends. I also often stand before larger groups of soldiers or churches, telling how Jesus Christ saved my soul—much like those early days of testifying at the open-air services. Looking back, I can see that God was preparing me then for what I would be doing later in life.

Likewise, Philip was being prepared for all that God had for him in Samaria, on the road to Gaza, in Azotus and on into Caesarea. Preparation time is never wasted time. How might God be preparing you now for what he might have for you in the future? How did you come into the Christian faith, and might that either have a connection with what you are doing for God now, or carry a clue as to what you might be called

Chapter 1

to do in the future? How could you learn from others you look up to in the faith, in order to glean wisdom for the calling which God has placed on you? Thankfully, we never 'arrive' at a place where we have our calling worked out perfectly so as to know exactly what to do in every situation. We are ever learning, growing, understanding and developing as workers in God's kingdom. This means that we are constantly reliant on the wisdom of God and his Word, and must continually lean on faith as we travel. It also means that we should glean insights from others—either from their living examples around us or from the works they have written. What might God be teaching you today for what he has for you tomorrow? What Philip was learning would pay off more quickly than he could have imagined.

NOTES

1   For more information on SASRA, visit http://www.sasra.org.uk.

Chapter 2

The scattering and the sending: God's role (and ours) in mission (Acts 8:1, 4)

For many years now, we in the West have suggested that the church, when under persecution, actually thrives. We say this because of the unexpected rise in Christian influence during the first- to fourth-century world: from a persecuted body of believers in Jerusalem to the Roman Empire's embrace of the Christian faith under the 'peace of Constantine' following the emperor's conversion in AD 312. We have also noted this principle in action over the last hundred years in countries such as China, Nigeria and the former Czechoslovakia, where, under threat of imprisonment or worse, the church of God has actually grown in the midst of the severest of trials. We have had the luxury of being onlookers at this historical and theological phenomenon.

However, it is not so today. Carter Conlon, Pastor of Times Square Church in New York City and successor to David Wilkerson, suggests that the church in the West is not currently under *persecution*, but under increasing *prosecution*. In the UK legal action has been taken against a bed-and-breakfast owner who refused a room to a gay couple in Marazion, Cornwall. Health-care workers have been brought before their bosses after offering to pray for suffering patients. An airline steward received complaints because she wore a cross. Open-air preachers have been charged with disturbing the peace because they have preached against sin. No, we are not yet in the throes of persecution as seen in Jerusalem at the time of the early church, or under threat of jail if we state our allegiance to Jesus Christ. Yet we may face prosecution for

Chapter 2

making a stand for our faith in these days. Let us always be ready to give a defence of our faith, as we are clearly called to do (1 Peter 3:15).

Philip, along with the others in the Jerusalem church, was beginning to feel the heat of persecution. He was most likely present in Acts 4 when, after the arrest and subsequent release of Peter and John for preaching in the open air about Jesus, the apostles gathered the church to pray—not for protection, favour or a peace-making strategy, but for boldness in the face of persecution! Their prayer was that God would 'look on [the authorities'] threats, and grant to Your servants that with all boldness they may speak Your word, by stretching out Your hand to heal, and that signs and wonders may be done through the name of Your holy Servant Jesus' (4:29–30). The divine response to this brave heart-felt and sobering prayer was such that 'the place where they were assembled together was shaken; and they were all filled with the Holy Spirit, and they spoke the word of God with boldness' (v. 31).

What a stand to take! They could so easily have decided to quieten down a little; to open dialogue with the Sanhedrin in order to create understanding concerning this growing group of Christians; and simply to whisper the name of Jesus to friends, if that would be acceptable. But their allegiance to Jesus their Lord and Saviour was worth more than staying quiet until the storm passed; more than trying to appease their persecutors through dialogue; more than whispering the name of Jesus. Their faith enabled them to be bolder, braver, stronger and louder than ever, for not only were they re-filled with the power of the Holy Spirit, but surely also they had these words of Jesus their Lord still ringing in their ears: 'Blessed are those who are persecuted for righteousness' sake, for theirs is the kingdom of heaven. Blessed are you when they revile and persecute you, and say all kinds of evil against you falsely for My sake. Rejoice and be exceedingly glad, for great is your reward in heaven, for so they persecuted the prophets who were before you' (Matt. 5:10–12). Persecution actually served to help the Jerusalem church focus on their

The scattering and the sending

purpose, to realize that they were storing up treasures in heaven by continuing to be witnesses for Jesus Christ, and that they would even see blessing as a direct result of their being reviled, criticized and even punished for their faith.

Acts 8 begins with the historical fact that, following the martyrdom of Stephen, there arose 'a great persecution' against the church in Jerusalem (8:1). There was not only a great persecution, but also a great scattering, and the church fragmented and began to be dispersed all over Judea and Samaria. The apostles remained in the city of Jerusalem, though, and from Acts 8, the early mission of the church begins to be centred on apostolic and evangelistic events beyond the great holy city and out to where Jesus said the message of the gospel should go: the ends of the earth.

We should at this stage consider the theological implications of those disciples who were scattered abroad as a result of the persecution of the Jerusalem church. The Greek word translated 'scattered' in Acts 8:1 is *diaspeiro*, from which we get the word 'disperse' or use it in its root meaning, 'diaspora'. The 'diaspora' are those who have been spread out, or, as the Greek language suggests, 'sown' or 'distributed'.

This is significant, as a casual reading of the text might suggest that the persecution simply produced a group of frightened and cowardly Christians running for safety. However, two observations need to be made. First, we have already seen that the church had prayed for boldness as a response to persecution, and they were living out a fearless witness in the city of Jerusalem. Was the power that filled them after the building-shaking prayer of Acts 4 suddenly impotent in the face of increased persecution? Second, the use of the word 'scattered' in Acts 8:1 suggests that the believers who left the city did not do so carelessly or in panic, but that they were 'sown' by God; they were 'distributed' according to his will.

The mechanics of this second observation can of course become a little muddy. We could go down the path of arguing the crossing point between

Chapter 2

the sovereignty of God and the will of human beings. The question which presents itself at this stage of the unfolding drama of Acts is this: Did those disciples simply leave the city out of fear, or were they sent out of the city with a purpose? Of course, one could simply say 'yes' to both. But does that help us in understanding the will of God in mission?

Much of the guidance in Scripture is directly transmitted: it follows the pattern of God speaking and human beings responding. Think of the calls of Abram in Genesis 12, Moses in Exodus 3, Gideon in Judges 6, or Samuel in 1 Samuel 3. God spoke, and these men responded. However, powerful and direct as God can be in calling his people to do a work for him, his calling can also be providential: circumstances can play their part. Think of Joseph. Did God call him to go to the prison where he would meet a butler and a baker, one of whom God would use to have Joseph released, not only to speak with Pharaoh, but to go on into a fulfilment of the prophetic dreams he had been given around thirteen years previously? He did not. He used the circumstances perfectly in order to arrange Joseph's release and promotion. Did God speak to David and tell him of the giant Goliath, who was defying the armies of Israel in 1 Samuel 17, so that he should go down to the battle and carry the giant's head from his shoulders? No, he did not. David was sent down to the battle to bring food for his brothers. There was no voice from heaven or direct calling to do anything. But when he saw the Philistine taunting the armies of God, he decided to act, and the rest is history: he defeated Goliath and there began a slow march into his destiny as king. God had promised, through an anointing by the prophet Samuel, that David would one day be king, but it was this act of bravery that catapulted David onto the national stage. He did it—but the action was undoubtedly orchestrated by God. Think also of Paul, converted and now beginning to preach in the city of Damascus—a city he was travelling to in order to persecute Christians, until he was met by the grace of God (Acts 9). Paul (or, as he was then still known, Saul) began immediately to preach in

Damascus, right after his conversion, but the Jews, who could not withstand him in the synagogues of that city, plotted to kill him. Saul's response? To be let down out of the city in a large basket in order to escape the Jews and certain death. Did God tell him to do that? Not that we read of; it seems he simply went along with the disciples' guidance and escaped. And yet, we can still see the hand of God in this action, preserving Paul for the world-changing ministry for which he was called and prepared. Sometimes guidance is providential and not so clear-cut.

This was the case with the scattering of the church at Jerusalem. The apostles were clearly going to remain in the city, for at least three reasons. First, they needed to disciple those believers who remained in the city. Second, had they left the city, this might have been perceived as a cowardly act. Third, had they left the city, they might have wondered whether they would miss the return of Jesus, as they lived their lives in the hope of his imminent second coming. But the great persecution against the church in Jerusalem was allowed to take place under the watchful eye of a God who had the nations in mind; of a God who had a purpose to spread the message of salvation through his Son's death on a Roman cross; and of a God who planned to use Philip in a very specific and dynamic way in order to see this mission come to fruition. Philip may have been 'scattered' from Jerusalem, but he was being guided in this dispersion to fulfil the mission for which God had called him, even from before the foundations of the earth (Eph. 2:10).

Whether he was fully aware of it or not at the time, Philip went out from Jerusalem on a mission from God and for God. His journey brings us to an important question: Is the work of gospel ministry to find out where God is working and to join in with that perceived spiritual movement? Or is the work of gospel ministry to initiate a work which we hope God will bless? In connection with this important question is the theological understanding of the '*missio Dei*'—the mission of God. *Missio Dei* is a contemporary buzz-phrase in the Western church which is rooted in the understanding that the mission we find ourselves in today as Christians is not actually to be termed 'the mission of the church', but, since our work for the kingdom of God originates with God himself, it should therefore be termed 'the mission of God'. This understanding then translates into the church navigating to places where God is presently at work in a local context and trying to join with his divine plan of action, rather than initiating a plan which originates with the local church within its context. On the surface, this posture sounds not only plausible, but also laced with humble spirituality, and who would not want to be humbly spiritual as a Christian? However, there are at least two difficulties with this theo-praxis, difficulties which cut across the biblical record of mission.

First, the biblical record of mission and of gospel ministry shows that those who engaged in this type of ministry were fantastically proactive. The apostle Paul, for instance, revealed a clear missionary zeal for the unreached people of the world. In other words, he was driven to go where there was clearly no visible work of God in action, but his very presence there initiated a gospel work. Why? Because he carried the presence of God with him and he preached and taught the Word of God in places where there was previously no understanding either of the identity of God as revealed in Jesus Christ, or of the salvific plan he had for the nations. Even a scant reading of the book of Acts demonstrates the pioneering activity of the gospel in an unevangelized area, rather than the sociological exegesis of a local context, and God blessed Paul's efforts. Second, the actual outworking of the contemporary understanding of the *missio Dei* is fast becoming more of a cultural compromise than a gospel engagement with the local context. For instance, this kind of practice is being played out in scenarios which resemble the following …

Recently, there was a tragic earthquake in Nepal that killed many thousands. Relief aid work is still underway, and many in the West have responded with financial giving and also in the sending of aid workers and supplies to Nepal. In the military barracks where I work as an evangelist to British Forces in Germany there have been several initiatives to raise money for those in severe need: for food, housing and medical care. A contemporary understanding of the *missio Dei* would be that, as social action is being carried out in the military barracks where I work, God must be involved there, working by his Spirit to cause human beings from one side of the world to help human beings on the other side of the world. This is then translated as God being at work in this activity, and therefore I must join in with this activity in order to be a part of the mission of God. That is how the *missio Dei* is being played out as a theo-praxis within many contemporary Christian contexts, and it is being hailed as the primary missiological approach to impacting the nations with the good news of the gospel. But is this biblical?

As I have stated, Paul did not dialogue with local leaders in order to find out where God might be working within a locality; he had an understanding of being sent to preach about Jesus the Christ to the main cities and towns of the known world of his day. Even at Mars Hill in Athens, where he did try to understand the cultural implications of the many gods there, his agenda was not to join in with the philosophies of the day and to glean wisdom for life; rather, he dissected the poetry and philosophy of the Greeks and from that dissection preached repentance, judgement and righteousness in their place (Acts 17:16–34). Likewise, after being filled with the Holy Spirit on the day of Pentecost, Peter did not conclude that, as Jerusalem was a religious city in which God must clearly be working at many levels anyway, there should be an engaging—a journeying together—with those in the city in order to discern what God might be up to. No, he boldly stood and proclaimed repentance, judgement and righteousness to the people of Jerusalem; and, as a result, thousands were converted.

As Philip was making his way to the city of Samaria, we can be assured that he was not intending to set up a base in the city from which to

Chapter 2

understand the moving of God. He did not arrive with plans to meet with local councils for dialogue concerning social ills; he did not desire to attach himself to social-action programmes in order to listen to the heartbeat of the city; he was not simply walking the streets trying to discern the will of God for his life. He had just come from Jerusalem, where he had seen mass conversions, miraculous divine interventions, a thriving church in spite of opposition and a growing church in spite of persecution. He had himself been used of God in the daily ministry of the church. Perhaps the main gospel weapons he carried as he travelled to Samaria were not past experiences, but the present reality that he was utterly committed to telling others about Jesus of Nazareth being the saving Son of the living God, and he was filled with the dynamite power of the Holy Spirit as he went. Samaria would soon discover that mission is indeed rooted in the mind and will of God, but this mission is not carried out by sociological experiments, anthropological insights or cultural appreciation. The mission of God is carried out by men and women who are committed to the message of the gospel; men and women who are filled with the Holy Spirit; men and women who dare to put their lives on the line for their Lord and Saviour, Jesus Christ.

Whose mission, then, are we involved in as believers today—is it the mission of the church or the mission of God? I would argue that the mission of the church *is* the mission of God, and vice versa. Acts 8:4 states, 'Therefore those who were scattered went everywhere preaching the word.' There is no sense here that those disciples who left Jerusalem were fleeing for their lives because of the name of Jesus. They went everywhere preaching the Word of God. What kind of preaching would this have been? As they would not have had time to go to theological college or gain academic qualifications, they most likely simply preached what they knew: 'There was a man called Jesus of Nazareth who claimed to be the Son of God, and who performed unquestionable miracles to prove his deity. This man died as a sacrifice on a cross, to pay for the penalty of sin in order to appease the wrath of a holy God. He died, was buried, and on the third day after his death was resurrected, later being seen by hundreds in the city of Jerusalem. This man will judge the living and the dead. Repent and be baptized for the remission of sins, and you will become the children of God. He will fill you with his Holy Spirit, empowering you to understand his Word, overcome temptation and be a witness of these things yourself.' I imagine that their preaching revolved around those major themes, for this is what Peter preached on the day of Pentecost, and what Philip, Paul and the other apostles preached as well.

No, those who were scattered did not have an understanding of the *missio Dei* as exegeting a local community and somehow being involved in order to understand the moving of God. They were convinced of the Saviour's identity; committed to the spreading of the gospel message; empowered by the flames of the Holy Spirit; and faithful to the commission of Jesus Christ—'Go into all the world and preach the gospel to every creature' (Mark 16:15). Philip travelled to Samaria with this intention.

From my experience as an evangelist, if I simply go somewhere to see what might happen, the regular outcome is that nothing happens: no opportunities to witness, no in-roads for the gospel, no testimony of God at work. Yet if I walk around the military barracks where I work, praying for God to send me to the right person or people; drop into a place where I know soldiers will be; or do my usual rounds of visiting the troops in their blocks in the evenings with gospel intentionality—then it should come as no surprise that God does open doors of opportunity; I do witness of the saving power of Jesus Christ; soldiers do talk to me about their souls. Philip went to the city of Samaria with gospel intentionality, ready to be a fiery servant for Jesus his Lord. Yes, he risked being imprisoned or worse, but he knew that God would bless him even under persecution, and, as happened for his friend Stephen, would also be with him should he have to pay the ultimate sacrifice for his faith. With Philip

Chapter 2

having that level of radical commitment in his mind, the message of Jesus on his lips and the fire of the Holy Spirit in his heart, we now trace his steps as he enters the city of Samaria.

Chapter 3

Philip the Evangelist: his message and ministry (Acts 8:5–8)

Acts 8:5 is striking in its brevity: 'Then Philip went down to the city of Samaria and preached Christ to them.' Had Philip simply been escaping the persecution which was taking place in Jerusalem, it might have made more sense for him to go somewhere very low-key and simply to blend into the local environment, hoping that issues of faith never came up in conversation. Perhaps a move into a smaller town or village, keeping himself to himself, might have been the preferred tactic. But not so for Philip: he travelled with determination to the city of Samaria, a city with inherent challenges for the potential gospel preacher.

The city is described by Howard Clark Kee and Franklin W. Young as being despised by the Jews because the Samaritans 'were thought to have mixed blood as a result of the forced mingling of races during the Assyrian occupation of Israel (eighth century BC)'.[1] The fact that Jews in Jerusalem already had difficulty with the message of the gospel reaching non-Jewish lands paves way for the utter scandal in this instance that not only are non-Jewish people being evangelized under Philip's ministry, but far worse—they are Samaritans! This is the revolutionary context into which Philip clearly intended to go. No, he was not running from the fires of persecution; in actual fact, he was running into the potential arena of martyrdom, arriving in this perceptibly dark city with a determination to preach the message of repentance.

We are told that Philip went down to Samaria and 'preached Christ to them'. Here we have the simplicity of the message of the gospel: it is the

Chapter 3

message of Jesus. As Jesus stood with the disciples before his ascension, he told them that they would be filled with the Holy Spirit and, as a result of this in-filling, they would be witnesses concerning him. They were not to be witnesses of the church, or of a pet doctrine, or of the Holy Spirit, or even of the authenticity of Scripture: they were to be witnesses of *him*.

How refreshing it is to hear an evangelist speak of Jesus Christ! Although many today claim to hold the title of 'evangelist'—and I am speaking specifically of those we might catch glimpses of on Christian television—I wonder how many could be singled out as being captivated with the clear calling of speaking of Jesus Christ and him alone? Many seem to be captivated with the need to validate their calling by claims of divine healing. Many others seem to have their ministry infected with a need to attach financial abundance to the message of the gospel. Still others openly affirm what seem to be little more than self-help steps towards being a better and more successful person. Is this really the call of the evangelist in action? Whatever happened to the biblical model—as displayed here in the life of Philip—of the evangelist as one whose primary task is to speak to the unbeliever of Jesus the Christ? Philip left Jerusalem and entered Samaria with one thing in mind: to preach Christ to the people! Here is a biblical principle which will be confirmed with our further insights into Philip's ministry: the work of the evangelist is to preach Christ!

This simplistic understanding of the ministry of evangelism in general and of the evangelist in particular is under scrutiny in our time. We live in an age when political, and therefore by default religious, correctness is the overriding cultural dictate and filter through which all beliefs, actions and ideas must pass. Clearly, a message as exclusive as that of Jesus Christ—that not only is he the only way to the only God, but also he demands a whole-hearted life commitment to the claims of the Bible concerning him—is a lot to accept in these religiously pluralistic days. As a result, many leaders in the Western church have decided to walk the path of accommodation in order to avoid offence and pejorative labels such as 'fundamental', 'conservative' or even 'narrow-minded'. A sure-fire way to avoid such labelling is to remove all offence. The result in our Western culture is that the speaking Christian is not as welcome in the public square as much as the social-action Christian is. In other words, if you as a Christian can be seen to plant gardens in areas of social depravation, or can help out at a food bank, or even become involved in the multi-faith initiatives which are gaining momentum, there will not be much of a social backlash. But if you come preaching Christ—beware! I wonder how Philip would be labelled in today's context. I don't think he would be received with gladness in the echelons of the social elite or in the corridors of local power! Seeing how Philip's ministry is recorded in Acts, he would easily qualify for the label of 'narrow-minded, fundamentalist bigot'. That is how our culture would view him. It seems, however, that God viewed him as an evangelist. Which opinion matters most?

The 'silent witness' posture is becoming increasingly the ecclesiological and missiological norm in our time. A phrase which has been falsely attributed to Francis of Assisi goes along the lines of 'Preach the gospel at all times; use words if necessary', and this has infiltrated the contemporary missionary psyche. In reality, Francis was a powerfully dynamic preacher of the gospel. In fact, preaching was his primary calling.[2] However, because of increasing pressure today from society, reports of legal action against those who make godly choices in the workplace, and a media portrayal which seems to denigrate all things Christian, the easier option is of course simply to toe the cultural line. But is this living as Scripture would require us to live?

Philip lived at a time which was of course very different from ours. But were the challenges of Samaria really that different from the challenges we face today? Samaria was a mixed-race city, a city with religious uncertainty and a deep-seated uneasiness about anything which came out of Jerusalem. Any sociological or anthropological study would have revealed that, on the surface at least, it was certainly not accepting of a

Chapter 3

radically exclusive message of ascetic life-change for a man who claimed to be God, and who seemed to have died at the hands of Romans, only to be raised to life again as an expression of his divinity and power. What kind of missionary committee would send a man into a context such as Samaria without first understanding and then highlighting the less than satisfactory missiological demographics of the area? From a human point of view, Philip should have stayed in Jerusalem! Thank God for the work of the Holy Spirit in guiding, prodding, leading, scattering, cajoling and herding us into our God-given opportunities! Human beings would look at Samaria and say that it was an impossible mission ground. God looked at Samaria and saw that it was ripe for revival! And Philip was ready and willing to be used in such a city.

Again, what was it that Philip preached to the Samaritans? Scripture tells us he simply preached Christ to them. The phraseology used is similar to Paul's when he confesses to the church at Corinth,

And I, brethren, when I came to you, did not come with excellence of speech or of wisdom declaring to you the testimony of God. For I determined not to know anything among you except Jesus Christ and Him crucified. I was with you in weakness, in fear, and in much trembling. And my speech and my preaching were not with persuasive words of human wisdom, but in demonstration of the Spirit and of power, that your faith should not be in the wisdom of men but in the power of God (1 Cor. 2:1–5).

Paul was clearly a master-builder when it came to the church of God. He knew what theology was and held doctrine to be highly important. He was educated at the feet of Gamaliel and was a highly intelligent man when it came to the classics of his time; at an intellectual level he could easily hold his own with anyone of his day. He could have portrayed himself as an intellectual to the Corinthian church, and impressed them to the point where he was held in high esteem and almost revered thanks to his excellent credentials and persuasive power. He could have ministered in such a way in that church. However, he made the crucial commitment to preach Christ to them: the crucified Christ. What did this mean for the Corinthians?

A cursory reading of Paul's first letter to the church at Corinth reveals that this was a church which, while undoubtedly spiritual and gifted, was nevertheless still full of pride, the flesh and self-will. Paul could easily have dissected the ills of this church and offered vistas of renewal, hope and recovery in response. What he chose to do instead was to preach Christ to them, and particularly the crucified Christ: a Christ who died physically, but who also died to the thought of taking the easier route, of fulfilling the lusts of the flesh for self-preservation, or of wanting to be hailed as important. Jesus Christ surrendered even to death on a Roman cross for the sin of the world, an act of grace the world did not deserve and still finds difficult to understand. The Corinthian church needed to hear this message. The Corinthian Christians needed to die to the thought that the most gifted people are the most important; that there is a hierarchy in the church; that sin can become an ally rather than an enemy. And so Paul preached Christ to them; the example, message and legacy of Christ were exactly what they needed to hear. They did not need a super-apostle or a larger-than-life preacher to indulge their flesh. They needed a servant to show them the way of the cross. That is the teaching they received, and it changed their church.

Similarly, Philip preached Christ to the Samaritans. There may have remained in Samaria a trace of knowledge concerning the Messiah after his conversation with the woman at the well of Sychar. Many people believed in Jesus as the Christ of God after Jesus spent two days in the area (John 4:39–42). Could it be that the sowing and reaping principle which Jesus spoke of in John 4 had direct reference to the future ministry of Philip in that region? It is certainly plausible. Whatever deposit of germinating faith was resident in Samaria by the time Philip arrived there, we know this: as soon as he arrived, he wasted no time in being

Chapter 3

employed as an evangelist right in the heart of the city. And as he preached, multitudes began to listen.

Acts 8:6–8 reveals a phenomenal and unexpected reaction as a result of Philip's preaching of Christ. For a start, Philip's preaching was characterized by the ability to engage with crowds—'multitudes', rather than just 'a multitude'. This suggests that there were multiple occasions of a multitude. The sense is given that, as Philip preached around the city, each time he preached on Jesus as the Christ of God and called those present to repent, the crowds swelled to hear him.

One of the inspirational facts we learn in the Christian classic *John Wesley's Journal* is that often, whether it was at 5 a.m. on a wet English morning, in the frost of winter or in areas of serious persecution, multitudes came to hear John Wesley preach.[3] There is no natural or logical explanation for that; it must have been the supernatural touch of God on his chosen vessel that caused thousands upon thousands to follow this small-statured, somewhat rebellious preacher up and down the length and breadth of the country. The same, of course, could be said of many others over the two millennia of the church: Patrick, Francis, Martin Luther, John Calvin, Jonathan Edwards, George Whitefield, William and Catherine Booth, Charles Spurgeon, W. P. Nicholson, Billy Sunday, Billy Graham, and many others who could be added to that list. The only valid explanation for multitudes coming to hear a preacher of the cross of Jesus Christ must finally rest on the sovereign choice and will of God. More so now, perhaps, than at any other time the church has seen grand orators, influential leaders, megachurch-builders, conference speakers and television personalities who speak to many people. But when you think of a pure gospel preacher, one who makes clear the challenges of repentance, judgement and righteousness, there is little logical reason why many thousands would come to hear someone like that. Yet God has proven not only that he *can* use a chosen vessel for this type of multitudes-ministry, but also that from time to time he actually *does*.

Philip the Evangelist

Not only did multitudes come to hear the Spirit-filled ministry of Philip, but they responded by heeding the 'things spoken by Philip, hearing and seeing the miracles which he did. For unclean spirits, crying with a loud voice, came out of many who were possessed; and many who were paralyzed and lame were healed' (8:6–7). Philip's ministry was the catalyst that led these multitudes to Jesus Christ in conversion. There was clearly a direct spiritual power emanating from Philip; this was no ordinary gospel campaign or meeting. God was working through Philip in a way which had traces of the ministry not only of the apostles back in Jerusalem, but also of Jesus himself.

We are told very specifically that in the midst of Philip's preaching of Christ to the city of Samaria, a confrontation was taking place in the realm of the supernatural. 'Unclean spirits' were coming out of many who had previously been bound by dark satanic forces. The fact that there could be demonic influence in the city should come as no surprise; later in the chapter we see that the city held in high esteem a magician—a worker of sorcery—by the name of Simon. This widespread allegiance to the dark arts (unlike the common sleight-of-hand trickery that goes under the name of 'magic' in our time) would have been an open invitation to evil influences, even to the point where if people gave themselves over to such powers, possession by those evil influences would follow. The biblical record informs us that 'many' were possessed.

This is almost a replaying of the work of Jesus in his own ministry. From this level of spiritual confrontation we can deduce that where there is a manifest, Spirit-filled servant of God confronting sin and calling for repentance and allegiance to Jesus Christ, those who might have sat at ease in their chosen darkness might suddenly be awakened to their spiritual blackness, oppression or even possession. We are cautious in using such words, as the professional world of psychology would no doubt baulk at terms such as 'oppression' and 'possession', preferring to attempt to cure the ills of humanity by counselling and various mind

Chapter 3

exercises. At a certain level, this may be helpful if the problem is a purely mental one. However, if there is a problem that is primarily spiritual, no amount of psychology will fix it. Such a problem can only be remedied by the power of Jesus Christ through the dynamic working of the Holy Spirit. I am painfully aware of cases which have hit the headlines in recent years concerning the apparent exorcism of children which amounts to little more than child abuse. This is not the scenario in Samaria. Nor was it the scenario in Jesus' ministry either, for Scripture tells us that simply with a word he caused evil spirits to come out of those who were possessed (Mark 5:1–20; Luke 4:31–37). There was no panic, seemingly no laying-on of hands, little drama: just a word. Jesus had the authority to carry out such a ministry. He also invested a measure of this authority in his apostles, and now this authority was being demonstrated in Philip as an evangelist. As Jesus did not highlight this aspect of his ministry but rather used it as a sign to point to the salvific mission he was employed in, so Philip would have followed his example and simply pointed his listeners to the fact that these things were happening to show that God is more powerful than evil, and that Jesus is the Christ, the Saviour, who came from heaven to earth to redeem the souls of men, women, boys and girls the world over.

We are also informed that 'many who were paralyzed and lame were healed'. Again, this is a direct replica of the ministries of Jesus and the apostles. Jesus' ministry is summed up in Matthew 4:23–25:

And Jesus went about all Galilee, teaching in their synagogues, preaching the gospel of the kingdom, and healing all kinds of sickness and all kinds of disease among the people. Then His fame went throughout all Syria; and they brought to Him all sick people who were afflicted with various diseases and torments, and those who were demon-possessed, epileptics, and paralytics; and He healed them. Great multitudes followed Him—from Galilee, and from Decapolis, Jerusalem, Judea, and beyond the Jordan.

We are told that this kind of ministry continued with the apostles, for after the day of Pentecost and the conversion of thousands in the city of Jerusalem, 'many wonders and signs were done through the apostles' (Acts 2:43). This demonstration of miraculous power from the hand of God continued through the evangelistic ministry of Philip.

Again, the miracles which Jesus performed acted as a signpost to the kingdom of God and as a divine identifier to the fact that he was the Son of God who had come into the world to save sinners. This same purpose was evident in the miracles performed by the apostles. For instance, the healing of the lame man at the Beautiful Gate in Jerusalem (Acts 3) served as a platform for Peter to preach the gospel and to challenge those present to repent (3:19). This was also clearly the case with Philip. Philip was first and foremost an evangelist rather than a worker of miracles. The miracles served to point to Jesus Christ, and it showed: multitudes followed Jesus Christ because of the preaching of Philip, rather than simply because of having watched a miracle show.

One of the outstanding aspects in the ministries of Jesus, the apostles and Philip is that the miracles which took place were instantly verifiable. If someone is completely lame (not just complaining of a painful leg) or totally paralysed (not just suffering from a severe cold), then, should a miracle take place, it will be undeniable: the lame person will be able to walk again (and stay walking), and the paralysed person will be physically restored (and will stay restored). The recorded miracles of the New Testament are far from dubious; the blind saw, the deaf heard, the paralysed were restored and the lame walked—or even leaped, as in the case of the lame man in Acts 3. Keen as I would be to see the same level of miraculous power present in the church today, I am afraid I do not see it. As someone said to me recently, 'I have yet to see an amputee healed.' This is a striking statement, as there would be no question of a miracle, were that to happen. But, as yet, there is no recorded instance of that

Chapter 3

having taken place, and the conflicts in Iraq and Afghanistan have sadly provided many young men with amputated limbs.

Does this mean that there is no healing in the church today? I would argue that there is. In James 5:14–15 we are told of a recovery process attributed to divine healing, in which the elders of a local church are to be called on to anoint the sick of the church with oil, and the prayer of faith will raise those sick people up. We are at least to pray for healing; the actual work of healing belongs to God and his will. There have also been records of genuine healing over the years of church history. The famous church historian Bede records healings accompanying the evangelistic work of Patrick, among others. Francis is said to have seen healings take place in his ministry; even John Wesley in his *Diary* records praying for the sick and seeing recovery, seemingly through divine power rather than through the simple natural recovery of time. So how are we to understand the apparent disconnect concerning the miracles of the first century and the apparent lack of such in our time?

First, we should take lightly the many dubious claims of healing on our television screens. Follow-up reports into the claims of those healed on stage at such events reveal fairly conclusively that the supposed healing lasts only for a little while and could be attributed to either adrenaline or hope at the time of the apparent miracle. Second, we must affirm that God is still a miracle-worker on many levels—in salvation; in the in-built healing of the body; in the birth of a child; in the recurring of the seasons, and the list could go on and on. Third, people do still get healed today. Yes, there is a mending that is due to medicine, but there is also a level of divine healing which does take place. Often this falls within the James 5-type, where elders or leaders of a local church pray fervently for the healing of a person and that healing, even in contradiction of expert medical diagnosis, does indeed take place and is sometimes even referred to by those within the medical profession as an act of God. I personally have been healed in such a way: I had torn my Achilles tendon and was unable to climb stairs, but, the day after prayer and the anointing of oil, I was able to run for fifteen miles pain-free. That is inexplicable. And the pain has never returned.

But what of Philip's ministry: could it be replicated again? Based on more recent church history, the obvious response would be 'No'. However, while I do not suggest that this kind of ministry will be seen once more in our day, if God saw fit to replicate it in our day, there is no person, inside or outside the church, who could stop him from doing so. This act of power would simply be down to the will of God and to him alone. No evangelist, minister, bishop, or even archbishop can dictate how God will move in our day.

One thing we are sure of, on the basis not only of Scripture but also of church history: God is still using evangelists to preach the gospel message with power, often to multitudes, and to multitudes who respond in faith. Let us pray that God would indeed raise up preachers like Philip, George Whitefield, D. L. Moody and Billy Sunday in our time. Cultural experts, anthropological studies and sociological surveys suggest that the West could not accommodate a preacher who preached to the masses in the way that Moody, Sunday and even Billy Graham did in the past. The suggestion is that we live in a different era, a different cultural setting. However, God is still the God who calls, equips and produces ministries to buck these cultural, anthropological and sociological observations. Perhaps the context we live in is actually the perfect scenario, just as Samaria was in Philip's time, for such a preacher—or preachers—to be called, anointed and sent by God once more.

NOTES

1. Howard Clark Kee and Franklin W. Young, *The Living World of the New Testament* (London: Darton, Longman & Todd, 1966), p. 196.
2. See, for instance, Julien Green's biography of Francis: *God's Fool: The Life and Times of Francis of Assisi* (London: Hodder & Stoughton, 1986).
3. *John Wesley's Journal*, abridged by Nehemiah Curnock (London: Epworth Press, 1949).

Chapter 4

The spiritual interface: confrontation on the devil's doorstep (Acts 8:6–24)

The city of Samaria, under the Spirit-inspired ministry of Philip, was stunningly responsive to the message of Jesus Christ as Lord, and, as a result, 'heeded the things spoken by Philip' (Acts 8:6). Philip's work impacted the city in such a way that the people were left, not ready to crucify, stone or assault him, but filled with 'great joy' (v. 8). No doubt the Samaritans, hearing a man of God from Jerusalem preach to them, might have expected a tirade of criticism, condemnation and judgement concerning their syncretistic lives. However, although Philip would have highlighted the reality of sin and its consequences, and of the impending judgement of a holy God, he nevertheless would also have stated that the message of the gospel is good news for the sinner, for it has the power to free the captive from the bondage of sin and to infuse the newborn saint with the Spirit of God for life and service. This message preached by Philip resulted in the city of Samaria being filled with joy. They must have sensed the presence of God in the life and ministry of Philip and realized that Philip was not on an isolated or confused trip, but that God must have sent him to them—to the Samaritans, a people who might have felt that they had fallen outside of the grace of God. God would surely bless the 'pure' ones in Jerusalem with the message of the Christ, but the Samaritans? Yet here was Philip, clearly on a mission from God, preaching this message of the kingdom to them. And how they received it!

If today we travelled around telling people that God sent his Son Jesus to die for the sins of the world, at best our hearers would raise an eyebrow and possibly think, 'That's nice.' Why would they think anything else? They certainly would not be filled with joy as a result. It would be like a doctor telling a man who has come in for a yearly medical check-up that a researcher in the USA has come up with the cure for lung cancer. The patient would most likely think, 'That's nice.' But how different the response would be if that same doctor had first told the patient that, having listened to his chest and heard his breathing, he suspected that cancer was present in that patient's lungs! Now everything is different! The man would be shocked at the news, but then, once the greater news of a lung-cancer cure had been reported, he would be filled with great joy! Similarly, the message of the gospel seems irrelevant to those who do not see their need of a gospel in the first place; the New Testament is clear about first showing people their need of a Saviour, and then, on the back of that information, revealing the remedy for that need: Jesus Christ.

When Jesus spoke to the woman at the well of Sychar in John 4, he revealed her sinful lifestyle before going on to reveal his identity as the Messiah, the Saviour. And she received this news with gladness. When Peter preached on the day of Pentecost in Acts 2, his stern condemnation of sin caused the gathered crowd to ask what they should do to be saved from the wrath of God, to which he replied that repentance and faith in Jesus Christ was the only remedy. When Paul addressed the Areopagus in Acts 17, he spoke of judgement and righteousness in order to prick the consciences of those philosophers who heard him. What good is the good news if no one believes that he or she is in danger? It is then not good news, but nice news; news that can be overlooked, ignored or even deemed totally irrelevant. The gospel is good news because it supersedes the bad news that sin infects every one of us and as such severs our relationship with God, meaning that judgement and ultimately hell await all who decide to remain in their sinful state. But the good news is that Jesus Christ took the punishment of the sin of the world on himself at the

Chapter 4

cross, and he now offers salvation, based on grace and acted on by faith, to all who believe. The gospel is good news to those who believe—those who see their sinful state and their need of salvation—but offensive news to those who are self-righteous or who wish to remain in their sin. The Samaritans understood that they needed the Saviour Philip preached about; they accepted that they were far from God and needed to repent in order to be redeemed; and this paved the way for the good news of the cross to penetrate their sinful hearts and cause them to become children of God. And they were filled with joy as a result!

Despite this city-wide conversion, it would be foolish to imagine Philip riding into the sunset as the all-conquering evangelist. When the kingdom of God is being demonstrated, when the power of God is being manifested, and when the gospel of Jesus Christ is being powerfully proclaimed and received, there should almost be an expectation that a spiritual backlash from devilish forces will inevitably take place. This is exactly what happened in the city of Samaria, as the figure of Simon came onto the revival scene.

Simon was known in the city of Samaria as the 'great power of God' (8:10). In order to receive such a moniker you would need to be a very spectacular type of person demonstrating spectacular types of sorcery, which Simon did demonstrate. At first, there seems to be a very clear-cut unfolding of the drama: Philip the Evangelist comes into town, preaches about Jesus with power accompanied by signs and wonders, many Samaritans believe his message, are baptized and start following this Jesus. Simon the sorcerer, the 'great power of God', also believes, is baptized, and follows Jesus Christ as his Lord and Saviour (v. 13). And everybody is happy, filled with joy, and there are no hiccups—until Simon becomes infatuated with the power of God.

There is no doubt that the conversion of Simon was real and genuine. Had it not been, then in every other place in Scripture where we read that someone 'believed', we would have to ask the question, 'But did that person really believe?' Acts 8:13 clearly states, 'Then Simon himself also believed; and when he was baptized he continued with Philip, and was amazed, seeing the miracles and signs which were done.' Simon believed the message that Philip preached, moved on from there to being baptized, and continued to follow Philip around, amazed at the power demonstrated through Philip's ministry. No red flag is being waved at this point in Simon's life; no alarm bells are sounded. Simon has found the Saviour, much like the rest of those in the city; he has become one of the converted.

However, when the apostles Peter and John arrive in the city and pray for the new believers to be filled with the Holy Spirit, Simon sees fit to offer them money in order that he too might be able to perform such a demonstration of power. Peter's rebuke in response to this request is both dramatic and cutting:

Your money perish with you, because you thought that the gift of God could be purchased with money! You have neither part nor portion in this matter, for your heart is not right in the sight of God. Repent therefore of this your wickedness, and pray God if perhaps the thought of your heart may be forgiven you. For I see that you are poisoned by bitterness and bound by iniquity (vv. 20–23).

What a response! Yet Peter was justifiably angry with Simon's proposition. Consider the context: Philip's ministry is dynamic, being responded to on a very large scale in the conversion of the Samaritans; it is accompanied by signs and wonders, and it is impacting the whole city. There is a serious infiltration of the kingdom of God into Samaria. Peter and John are there to verify this, to encourage the new believers, and to see them grow in the experience of the Holy Spirit. Hot on the heels of this growth comes a man who was once renowned in the whole city for his sorcery and 'great power', asking if the real great power of God might be purchased. Samaria was a city that was used to supernatural activity,

Chapter 4

and Simon was the man who had been at the helm of this activity. Had Simon been allowed to remain in his misguided understanding that this new power was simply another way to become famous or revered in Samaria, then all the holy work that was being carried out by Philip and the recently arrived apostles could have become diluted, and syncretistic. Peter needed to nip this understanding in the bud and challenge Simon to give up the idea that the power of God can be bought or is available to make anyone famous. He sternly rebuked Simon for Simon's own personal good, for the wider good of the city, and to protect the ongoing work of God in Samaria.

Did Simon lose his salvation in the making of this request? No, he did not. Peter's statement that Simon's heart was not right concerned the matter of his request, not his standing before God. If we were to lose our salvation because of mistakes we made shortly after conversion, who would be a Christian today? We have all made mistakes, and we continue to make them, not just in the fledgling days after conversion but even decades after. Thank God that he is a forgiving God! Peter says as much in calling Simon to repentance and revealing that God is a God who forgives the truly penitent. Should it really be a surprise that Simon still had traces of his old life going into his new-found faith? Did you not still have areas of your old life trying to remain alive as you entered into the life that Jesus gave you? Are you not still taking a stand in your life today to remain in Christ, rather than go back to the old person you used to be before Jesus rescued you? The struggles that even the apostle Paul speaks of in Romans 7 are real for all of us, and it was the same for this man Simon. He was yet to be educated on the difference between holy and unholy power; yet to understand that we are to decrease while Jesus Christ in us increases; yet to know that there is no gain in having the whole world and yet losing our own soul. Yes, Peter was straight with him—arguably more straight than many pastors in our churches today would be—but it was a necessary rebuke, considering the intent of Simon's heart and the budding work of God in Samaria.

Simon had been converted under the ministry of Philip, but he still held onto traces of his old, dark life. This could have provided an opening for the powers of darkness to work through, in order to upset the work of God in Samaria. I have little doubt that the plan to undermine or abort this revival came from a satanic plot against the kingdom of God, against the budding of a vibrant, Christ-centred church in a city where once the 'great power of God' was actually a man who was such an expert in sorcery that the whole city was in awe of his spiritual power. How did this spiritual confrontation play out to the point where Simon became sorrowful concerning his actions, and the work of God continued? It did not involve politics; it did not involve placards and demonstrations; it did not involve physical aggression; it did not involve name-calling and condemnation. It was settled because a man of God, under the unction of the Holy Spirit, spoke prophetically into Simon's heart and demanded that he repent, or he would find himself under the judgement of God, even as a newborn saint. There was no debate, no dialogue, no compromise. God spoke through Peter and left Simon with only two choices: repent or be judged. From Simon's response, we can only hope he chose repentance (8:24).

The arrival of the Enlightenment led to the rise of apologetic preaching, as can be seen in the lives of the Oxford graduates John Wesley and George Whitefield in the eighteenth century, and we in the twenty-first century still maintain a measure of apologetics as a foundational approach to dealing with repentance, be it with the unconverted or the converted. Apologetics is the practice of intellectual and logical argument which, concerning the gospel, is employed in the hope of persuading the listener mentally to weigh up the facts as a pathway to accepting the merits of biblical truth. In the wake of the Enlightenment we can see the providential guidance of God in steering both Wesley and Whitefield

Chapter 4

towards a robust academic education, such that these two preachers developed an educated posture in preaching the gospel, in order to reach an increasingly educated audience. But has preaching the gospel moved even further towards the demands of an educated Western world and forsaken the apostolic preaching which, empowered by the Spirit of God, sought to cut the people to the heart with the Word of God, instead simply becoming 'educated' in its apologetic approach?

I am not arguing against apologetics; a sound and intelligent reasoning with others concerning the merits of the gospel has its place. God has used many intelligent people in church history to be preachers of the gospel of Jesus Christ. Neither am I arguing for a widespread boycott of Christian theological training in our universities. As I write, I am nearing the end of a doctorate on postmodern evangelism, having also obtained an MA and a BTh from English universities. How can I repudiate academic study when I have walked that path myself? What I am concerned about, however, is how academic study is translated into practice. Is our qualification to minister for God to be found in the printed certificate of a university degree, or is it to be found in the recesses of eternity under the calling and equipping of God? Yes, we can argue that it should be both—under God and in the sight of people; but when it comes to priority, there should be no even balance: the qualification of any minister of God comes from the mind and commissioning of him who called us, and, in this regard, university or Bible college qualification comes nowhere near that level of affirmation.

Because of an unbiblical acceptance of the academy as holding primary importance in theological qualification, preaching the gospel in our time has become a vehemently apologetic, educated, intellectual, and at times aloof practice. It has seemingly 'progressed' from the days when the apostles were known to be unlearned, uneducated men. But where has this swing towards the academy taken us? Has it really, by means of a better education and an apologetic approach, caused multitudes to come rushing into the kingdom of God, as they did in Jerusalem or in Samaria? We need to understand that if we are to be truly biblical preachers of the gospel, we must lay down any idea we have of intellectually winning anyone into the kingdom of God. It will not happen. Our mandate from Jesus himself was never to develop our intellects so that we might win the lost, we might better understand Scripture, we might learn new riches for our personal devotional lives, or we might improve the theological understanding of those we lead. Our academic rigours will not sway anyone to become a believer in Jesus Christ. That work is a work of the Word of God as preached under the inspiration of God, and the apostles and Philip have given us examples of how to carry out such preaching: by reaching for the heart of the unbeliever; by preaching repentance, judgement and righteousness; by preaching the cross of Jesus Christ. This kind of preaching may not cause the Christian television stations to come calling or propel the preacher of the cross onto the covers of Christian magazines, but it will penetrate the hearts of the unconverted the world over and will give those who hear such preaching the chance to decide whether to repent or to turn away. We are not called to deliver three-point alliterated sermons, sermonettes, homilies, presentations, funny stories, moving images, or to use any other technique which we have become used to in our increasingly postmodern era. We are called to preach the Word. Philip threw himself headlong into obeying this mandate in Samaria, and multitudes were touched by the power of God—even to the point that the dark sorcerer Simon became a follower of Jesus Christ.

Apologetics did not win the city. Academics did not win the city. The only way this city was won for the kingdom of God was because a man, filled with the Holy Spirit, went into Samaria with the call ringing in his heart to preach the gospel to every person, and was willing to die for his faith and to lead those who would listen into repentance and faith in the Son of the living God. If Jesus' cross is still as potent now as it was then,

Chapter 4

and if the human heart is as in need of salvation now as it was then, how can we decide to preach in any way other than by following the example we have in Scripture? Even when confrontation at a spiritual level arose to challenge this great work of God in Samaria, a strong reliance on the true power of God, the sense of authority given to the child of God, the elevation of Jesus Christ and his Word, and the clear, unashamed challenge of repentance overcame what could have been a stemming of revival. The tactics of the powers of darkness were thus thwarted, the work of God prevailed, and Philip was about to receive another appointment.

Before we see Philip head towards the desert road, let us consider the arrival of Peter and John in Samaria, and see how a multi-gift ministry consolidates and helps the work of God.

Chapter 5

Establishing the disciples: multi-gift ministry (Acts 8:14–17)

Philip could have become very upset when Peter and John came down to Samaria from 'headquarters' in Jerusalem to assess the work of God in that city. If you have been around churches for a while, and, in particular, if you have become close to ministers or are a minister yourself, you will understand that people can become not only incredibly territorial concerning their work for God, but also very protective of it. How often have you heard the term 'one-man ministry' used in pejorative terms? Maybe you know quite a few of those. Maybe you are one!

The first observation we should make regarding this scenario is this: Philip was a man of God. He was a servant, he could negotiate disputes well (as we saw regarding the widows in Jerusalem), he was filled with the Holy Spirit, he had a good reputation in the church, he went down to Samaria, he was a powerful preacher, he saw a genuine revival with multiple conversions, and he was a faithful evangelist. What more could a man of God hope for in his ministry? We might ask whether he really needed supervision from Jerusalem. The answer I would give to that searching question is a resounding 'Yes!'

No matter how much of a man of God Philip was—and certainly no matter how gifted he was, and no matter what kind of successes he was having in Samaria—Philip was, ultimately, limited, and in at least three ways. First, he was limited in his gifting. Yes, Philip was an evangelist; yet an evangelist may be good at many things, but he will not be good (or

Chapter 5

gifted) at everything. He could preach the gospel, be used supernaturally, even confront evil—but there is a lot more to making disciples than this. It is possible to have the double gifting of, for example, evangelist-pastor, or evangelist-teacher, but Scripture does not tell us that Philip had this level of gifting; he was an evangelist. Yes, he was a revival-evangelist, but still he was limited. He needed others to come alongside him and, with their spiritual gifts, help to establish these new believers.

Second, he was alone. Again, no matter how dynamically gifted a person may be, it is not good for that person (in the work of Christian ministry) to be alone. Aloneness can provide many hurdles in the work of the gospel. It can lead to isolation, burnout, depression, pride, a maverick attitude, biblical compromise, biblical error, laziness or even apostasy. In extreme circumstances, God may allow a period of aloneness in Christian ministry for a specific season, but long periods of isolation in gospel work can begin to open the minister up to all kinds of distractions or temptations. Jesus himself was left alone in the wilderness to be tempted by Satan for a period of forty days. Yet, once that isolation period was over, not only did the angels come and minister to him, but also he began to call others to come and be a part of his work. It is not good for a Christian worker to be alone for a long period of time.

Third, Philip was on the frontline of spiritual battle. He was in the arena facing a horde of gladiators, and he was on his own in the fight. Of course, others were becoming Christians and joining the kingdom of God, and this was a joy in the city; but those new converts needed nurturing and spiritual feeding, and they were a target for spiritual attack themselves in those early days. They needed to be established in their new-found faith. Philip was preaching the gospel across the city, and was busy enough keeping up with the revival that was divinely under way. The evangelist's cry is 'Souls, souls, souls!' But what about those newly converted souls? They needed more than an itinerant evangelist for them to become established in their faith.

Establishing the disciples

Given these three areas—Philip's limited gifting for the establishing of a body of new believers in Samaria, the potential dangers of being alone in ministry, and with him being the target in spiritual warfare—we can see the grace of God in sending Peter and John down to Samaria not only to see what was happening, but also to help Philip in this revival work.

Evangelists today face the same issues. I write this as an evangelist myself, working in a British military context. The work is exciting; it is an immense privilege; it has seen outstanding blessing. Yet I am aware of my limitations. For instance, I am very comfortable preaching the gospel to a hundred soldiers in a military church service. I am happy visiting men in their barrack blocks in the evenings to strike up gospel conversations with them. I am content in giving out Christian literature and resources on British Army camps. However, I would find dealing with church committees incredibly tedious. I would experience a measure of frustration in counselling Christians over a long period of time in order to help them make life changes. I would not relish the thought of living my life and carrying out my ministry among a specific number of Christians in the extremely localized context of a local church. All these factors point to the reality that I am not a pastor! I can be pastoral, and I have served as an interim pastor for two years, but it is not my life's calling. I would much prefer to face a hundred soldiers with the gospel than face a church committee to go over the yearly financial projection for the upcoming budget! In other words, I am limited in my work. Thankfully, we have chaplains and other Christians in the British military who also put their shoulders to the work and together we carve out a work for God on the camps where God has placed us.

The contemporary evangelist can also operate alone. This is not a positive attitude in gospel ministry. No matter how gifted an evangelist may be, that evangelist needs to be part of a local church with accountability to local leadership. Evangelists have, unfortunately yet often justifiably, been seen in the past as mavericks in the church at large.

Chapter 5

Why should an evangelist who is seeing conversions regularly, and filling churches or even larger buildings, submit to the pastor of a local church with possibly only around fifty or a hundred people in attendance each week? There are at least two reasons why he should. First, pastors are to look after the flock of God, and no matter how qualified, gifted or famous an evangelist may be, the evangelist is still a member of the flock of God and needs to be shepherded. Second, an evangelist operating alone without accountability can end up in all sorts of trouble—sin, false doctrine, pride and financial issues, to name just a few. The evangelist under authority is a better, more humble, more accountable evangelist. If there is anything the church does not need, it is more fallen evangelists! The evangelist needs the local pastor, not only in the work of the gospel, but also for personal accountability.

The contemporary evangelist is on the frontline of spiritual battle. This has not changed in two thousand years. The work of the evangelist takes place at the spiritual interface where the gospel is delivered to the unbeliever. This can be a painless process, but equally it can involve a serious measure of spiritual confrontation. If the evangelist is alone in this battle, without the help of a pastor and of other ministry gifts in the body of Christ, the evangelist is the sole target for spiritual attack.

When I was a soldier in the British Army, I worked a lot in Northern Ireland and we had various drills in how to engage rioters in a riot situation. The one thing that was never an option was to allow any one soldier to become isolated at any time. Why? Because an isolated soldier is an easy target for rioters and could very quickly end up injured or worse. In a normal riot scenario, we would advance or maintain ground in set formations, all rehearsed around the protection of others and our own soldiers. However, in extreme circumstances—such as when petrol bombs would be hailing down on us, or the bricks were coming at us in greater volume—we would adopt a position known as 'the shell'. You can see a form of this in the movie *Gladiator*: it is when the attack is so

Establishing the disciples

severe that the soldiers interlock their riot shields to form an impenetrable shell. A soldier who is alone cannot withstand such an attack, and it is the same with evangelists. I urge all evangelists or those involved in evangelism to seek out, at the very least, a godly pastor under whom to serve and to whom to be accountable, and, if possible, a larger team of others to serve alongside in the work of the gospel. There is too much at stake for the evangelist to become injured or worse, simply because that evangelist operated alone.

When John Wesley began to be mightily used of God in the villages, towns and cities of the UK in the mid-eighteenth century, he could easily have simply preached the gospel, had many converts, and left for the next destination. Rather than do that, Wesley began to develop 'societies' of believers. These societies would be the foundation blocks for the Methodist denomination. He understood that these societies needed leaders and teachers so that new converts could be discipled in their faith. An itinerant evangelist, even one as great as Wesley, could not do this work alone. Also, on his many travels he made the wise decision to meet with his brother Charles, the famous Christian hymnwriter, as often as he could, and also to stay with like-minded Christian ministers, lay leaders, or members of the laity. This was not only a wise lifestyle choice, but also a protective one. Even Wesley needed to be careful as an evangelist.

Likewise, the apostle Paul, as a preacher of the gospel, saw conversions in many towns and cities on his missionary journeys. Yet he decided to appoint elders (pastors) in every local church, because even his ministry alone could not establish these new converts. Also, when he travelled he took others with him: Barnabas, Timothy, John Mark, Silas and others. He was not a maverick, even though he could easily have become one. He chose to be a team-ministry apostle, not a one-man 'super-apostle'. If Jesus, Paul, Philip, Wesley and others God has used powerfully in the church's past did not feel it best to work alone, then we should see that in

Chapter 5

the arrival of Peter and John in Samaria, God was working for the best interests of all concerned: for the evangelist, for the converts, and even for Simon the sorcerer.

Philip welcomed the apostles in Samaria and straight away they began to get involved in establishing the new converts in the city. The first step we see them take in Acts 8:15–17 is that they 'prayed for them [the Samaritan converts] that they might receive the Holy Spirit. For as yet He had fallen upon none of them. They had only been baptized in the name of the Lord Jesus. Then they laid hands on them, and they received the Holy Spirit.'

We know for sure that the city of Samaria 'had received the word of God' (v. 14). There is of course hyperbole here, for the text is clearly not suggesting that every single person—man, woman, boy and girl—had become a Christian. Later, Acts 17:6 suggests that Paul had 'turned the world upside down' with the teaching of Jesus as the Christ of God, and it is the same kind of language that is used here to describe the level of impact which the gospel was having in Samaria. There were enough converts to suggest that the whole city was at least being affected by the gospel message. Now we know that there were already many converts in the city, not simply because there was healing, deliverance, preaching, joy, and city-wide acknowledgement that this message which Philip preached was true, but also because we are told in 8:12 that many believed the message Philip shared and 'both men and women were baptized'. As far as we read in Scripture, no one was baptized into the Christian church unless there had been repentance of sin, an acknowledgement of Jesus as Lord, and therefore evidence of a real born-again, new-life-giving, redemption-giving, righteousness-imputing faith. These new disciples were, however, to receive a promise which had already been evidenced in the city of Jerusalem and of which Peter and John were experts.

Acts 2 records that in the upper room in Jerusalem on the day of Pentecost, the believers were waiting for the coming of the Holy Spirit as promised by Jesus (Acts 1:8). When the Holy Spirit did come as a rushing, mighty wind, the believers were all filled, began to speak in languages they did not previously know, and went out into the streets of Jerusalem, where Peter spoke to the gathered multitude. Here we have the coming of the Holy Spirit as a distinct event after those who were present had already confessed Jesus as Lord and had trusted in him for salvation. However, this was the arrival of the church age, and we should not build any doctrine based on one episode, as any good theologian would agree. One conclusion we can come to based on the Acts 2 account is this: that the Holy Spirit moves men and women to witness for Jesus Christ with a renewed boldness and with supernatural spiritual strength.

Likewise, in the prayer of Acts 4 following the arrest of Peter and John, the gathered church prayed for boldness, for God to display signs and wonders to demonstrate his power, and also for a renewed ability to continue to preach the word of God concerning Jesus. The building then physically shook, and 'they were all filled with the Holy Spirit, and they spoke the word of God with boldness' (4:31). Here is more evidence of the filling of the Holy Spirit. The outcome of both the Acts 2 and Acts 4 fillings was the preaching of the word of God, the disseminating of the gospel. And now in Acts 8, the city is being touched by the Holy Spirit and a divine power is spreading throughout the Samarian church, causing the witness of lives changed through the preached gospel message to permeate the city.

We need to remember that the only biblical account of the church of the living God suggests that it is a Spirit-filled church; so, if we are to be a biblical church, we should also be a church that is filled and anointed by the Spirit of God. There has been many a theological debate concerning the role of spiritual gifts in the church today, but there is a viable argument, based on the Acts account, that perhaps the strongest evidence of a believer being filled with the Holy Spirit is not the producing of a spiritual gift but having the boldness to witness for Jesus Christ, together

Chapter 5

with a life which is increasingly sanctified, as by the Spirit of the living God. The biblical record gives evidence of a Spirit-filled church; and if we as a contemporary church are to be biblical at all, we must seek to be continually filled with the Spirit of God in order to be not only faithful witnesses of the gospel, but effective ones too.

The account in Acts tells us that once someone was filled with the Holy Spirit, something happened: whether it was a supernatural ability to preach the gospel with power; a new, divine boldness not experienced before; the ability to confront evil; or simply the divine effusion of joy—something happened! As stated earlier, the early church had power—but the contemporary church has PowerPoint. Given how the early church, under the influence of the Holy Spirit, had great boldness in witnessing, it is logical to conclude that if the powers of darkness could remove this desire to be continually filled with the witnessing power of the Spirit of God, they would remove the fire of evangelism from the church—that passionate drive to tell others about Jesus Christ with some authority. Imagine what the contemporary Western church would look like if it was filled with a burning passion to see lost souls won for the King of all eternity! We need only read the book of Acts to see what disciples filled with God's Spirit are capable of. Why not pray that you and your church might experience the gospel zeal of the Holy Spirit—and then see what the Lord will do with you, with your church, and consequently with your town or city!

Chapter 6

From the spotlight to the shadows: radical obedience to radical guidance (Acts 8:26–40)

So everything is going better than it might ever have been expected to go. Following the diaspora from Jerusalem, Philip has arrived in Samaria and begun, with signs and wonders, to preach to the Samaritans about Jesus the Christ. They do not persecute him; on the contrary, they receive him and his words, believe in the message he preaches, are baptized, and, after Peter and John's visit, are filled with the Holy Spirit. Not only is the power of sorcery under Simon broken in the city, but the city is actually filled with joy as a result of Philip's ministry. It looks as if Philip is well set for a long and illustrious ministry in the city!

Peter and John now leave Samaria, having preached and testified there, and they continue to preach the gospel in many of the Samaritan villages on their return journey to Jerusalem. All is well with the work in Samaria, and perhaps they have planned another trip to visit Philip there in the near future, or maybe even to let some of the others in Jerusalem go down to Samaria for a persecution-free time of preaching, teaching and being blessed in the process. Surely it would do some of the other apostles good to get out from under the oppression of Jerusalem and see real revival fruit in Samaria without the risk of arrest or being beaten. Those are good plans, are they not? Yet sometimes the plans of humanity and of God are radically different.

Chapter 6

We read in Acts 8:26 that, seemingly unexpectedly, an 'angel of the Lord spoke to Philip, saying, "Arise and go toward the south along the road which goes down from Jerusalem to Gaza." This is desert.' We need to take a moment just to let that sink in. If there was anyone who should leave the city of Samaria, surely the last person chosen should have been Philip. Why not choose some of the new converts who might be showing promise in gospel work? Why not an understudy of Philip's? What about those who needed to be nurtured in the faith—what would they do without Philip's steadying influence? I have no doubt that these questions presented themselves to Philip, and, had Philip shared his plans with others in the community of faith in Samaria, no doubt they would have had those same questions too. We are not given any detail as to the questioning process, the wrestling with God process, or the communication with the new Christian leaders in Samaria. We are simply told that Philip got up and left. Just like that. People are being healed, demons are being cast out, multitudes are being baptized, Peter and John have no doubt gone back to Jerusalem with a glowing report, Philip has, under God, made the city joyful—and now he is told to leave it all behind. Which leaves us with one very solid conclusion: God knows what he is doing, even when we do not.

When someone enters some form of Christian ministry, one thing should be established right at the outset: it is God who is in charge of the work, not us. God has greater knowledge, further vision, deeper compassion, wider understanding and higher love than any of his chosen subjects. It must be settled at the beginning of the minister's journey that obedience to God will sometimes make us carry out orders simply because of the One who is giving them, and not because we understand why they were given. We see that the apostle Paul was not happy with being forbidden to preach in Asia (Acts 16:6). Who, as a gospel preacher, would not be upset when doors seem to be closed to the gospel message? Yet we are told that it was God who closed the door, and not only to Asia, but to Bithynia too (16:7). Why would God do such a thing? It is not for us necessarily to have the answers as soon as we ask; it is not wrong to ask, so long as we are prepared to wait for God to respond in his own time. As it turned out, God's plan was for the gospel to travel north-west rather than north-east, and into mainland Europe.

Have you had experiences where doors seemed closed to you, no matter what you tried to do, even for the gospel? Looking back, perhaps you can trace the hand of God in those closed doors, as God led you on a different path, in order to fulfil the plan he had for your life—a better plan than the one you had. Isaiah 30:21 assures us that when we take a step, God's voice will be 'behind you, saying, "This is the way, walk in it," whenever you turn to the right hand or whenever you turn to the left'. This verse suggests that a person has already taken steps, for the voice is behind, not in front calling that person forward. Even when we make steps in a wrong direction, God, as he did with Paul, will still direct us by his divine guidance.

Philip was busy in a revival town when God spoke to him and called him to leave the city and go to a desert road. He was leaving the spotlight and heading towards the shadows. Yet, free from the potential adulation of the Samaritans, free from the affirming words and reputation he would have had among the apostles, and free from his own potential ambitions, Philip left the relative ministerial fame of leading a revival in order to slip into seeming obscurity on the Gaza road. If there was ever an example of radical obedience to radical guidance, this was it. I wonder, would I do the same? Would you? Philip gives us a stunning example of how to follow God, whether before multitudes or before no one. He seemed to live his life only for the pleasing of the One who called him to salvation; Jesus of Nazareth, the Son of the living God.

As he journeys down towards Gaza, he comes upon a chariot, which would most likely have been part of a caravan of travellers returning to Ethiopia. Philip must have seen the chariot, for the Spirit of God spoke to

Chapter 6

him and said, 'Go near and overtake this chariot' (8:29). Philip, ever the obedient evangelist, ran over to the chariot and began to listen to the man travelling in it, a eunuch from Ethiopia, reading aloud from the prophet Isaiah. Now perhaps he understood the journey from Samaria and why he had to leave. He would understand more as he found out the identity of this reader from Africa.

Philip asks the eunuch whether or not he understands what he is reading. The Ethiopian replies by saying that he needs help to understand the meaning of the passage and who Isaiah is speaking of in these words:

He was led as a sheep to the slaughter;
And as a lamb before its shearer is silent,
So He opened not His mouth.
In His humiliation His justice was taken away,
And who will declare His generation?
For His life is taken from the earth.

This passage, taken from the mighty fifty-third chapter of Isaiah, is then preached by Philip, and Jesus is revealed as the central figure of the text (Acts 8:35). Philip had continued the ministry he began in Samaria when he preached Jesus to the multitudes; now he is preaching Jesus to one man.

The drama unfolds as they continue travelling, for as they pass by some water the eunuch asks whether there is anything that might hinder him from being baptized. Philip, making sure that he does not baptize someone who has not made a firm salvific commitment, says that there is a hindrance: only those who believe in Jesus with all their heart can be baptized (v. 37). The Ethiopian responds by stating, 'I believe that Jesus Christ is the Son of God.' The Ethiopian having stopped the chariot, Philip takes him into the water, and, just as he had done with so many in the city of Samaria, he baptizes him. Philip is then called away again by the Spirit of God on another mission, and the Ethiopian eunuch continues his journey rejoicing.

Not only is Samaria changed under the power of the gospel and filled with joy, but so is this man from Africa: a man 'of great authority' (v. 27) in the treasury of Queen Candace, the ruler of Ethiopia. Could it be that Philip had been used not only to preach the gospel to the Samaritans as a revolutionary missionary, but also to introduce the gospel message of Jesus the Christ into the further regions of the great continent of Africa?

The true evangelist, like Philip, is happy to share the gospel with the multitudes or with the individual. Of course, the exciting work is to lead large numbers of people into the kingdom of God rather than to be concerned about the ones and the twos. Yet Philip's evangelistic work was not about increasing his own fame, career or ministry. It was carried out under the specific orders of a God who cared not only for the multitudes of Samaria, but also for one lone traveller to Ethiopia. Yes, this one conversion, through the gospel seed of this one eunuch, might in time have led to the conversion of many in Ethiopia—but Philip was not sent to Ethiopia. He was sent to a eunuch of high estate so that this man could be a witness to his own people. We might wonder how a brand-new convert to the Christian faith could possibly have such an impact on his own people, young in the faith as he was. But we need to understand that God is in charge of guiding his people, whether by open doors or closed ones, and he is also in charge not only of saving the sinners, but also of keeping the saints. Philip could have tried to run after the Ethiopian eunuch and made sure he was at least a little stronger in the faith before he arrived in his homeland. But God saw fit not only to remove Philip from the scene, but to remove him immediately. This again tells us that God is our best guide, and, as in the case of the Ethiopian traveller, our best keeper too.

Perhaps you have preached the gospel to someone who has either responded favourably or made a solid commitment to follow Jesus as

Chapter 6

Lord and Saviour. Have you then, due to the circumstances at the time, had to let that person go on his or her way, leaving you wondering about that person's salvation? Perhaps many of us have had to do that at times. This encounter between Philip and the Ethiopian encourages us with the knowledge that God can not only save someone soundly in an instant, but can also keep that person as well—even without your continuing influence.

Someone must have been handing out gospel tracts in Belfast one day when my friend came walking by. There were still a few tracts lying on the ground, and he decided to pick one up. He had just been released from a youth remand centre, having stabbed someone in a fight and served his time. Now he was on his way home. He read the tract as he went, and once he arrived, he prayed to God, asking him if he really was there and was the kind of God described in this tract. God saved my friend as a result of that prayer, without the distributor of that gospel tract even being aware of it! It is God's work not only to save, but to keep as well.

Philip baptized this Ethiopian eunuch and was immediately called away on another journey—one that saw him first arrive in Azotus, and then go back on the road as an itinerant evangelist. Yet his work would not end in this way: God had even more surprises for this radically obedient man of God.

Chapter 7

Itinerant and static: Philip's evangelistic ministry as model (Acts 8:40)

It was the providence of God that allowed a higher level of persecution to hit the believers in Jerusalem, resulting in the widespread dissemination of the gospel message to the surrounding areas outside the great city. We read that this took place as a 'scattering' of disciples, suggesting that it was a chaotic response to the widespread attacks that took place on Christians in the city. Yet, as we have scratched beneath the surface, we have seen that these disciples went everywhere preaching about Jesus being the Christ, the Saviour sent from God. Philip was one of those scattered and was led by divine purpose into the city of Samaria. What then unfolded as recorded in Acts 8 was nothing less than the mighty hand of God using a devoted and Spirit-filled man to impact a city for the gospel in a way that has rarely been replicated throughout church history. This obedient man then obeyed the strange order to leave the revival and go towards the desert—a big ask, but a wise one in retrospect, as he led an Ethiopian official to salvation, baptizing him on the journey, before being whisked away in order to continue his evangelistic endeavours.

We take up his story in the very last verse of Acts 8: 'But Philip was found at Azotus. And passing through, he preached in all the cities till he came to Caesarea' (v. 40). When Philip first left Samaria under the direct order of God, he travelled south-west towards Gaza and towards the Mediterranean Sea. En route he had his encounter with the Ethiopian, and then he was found at Azotus, which is around twenty miles north of

Chapter 7

Gaza, following the coastline. We are then told that Philip began to journey even further north towards Caesarea, which is approximately fifty miles further north from Azotus, again along the coastline of the Mediterranean. As he travelled, he stopped off at 'all the cities' along the way. We are not told specifically which cities he stopped at, but there is every possibility that he could have visited Emmaus, Lydda, Joppa, Arimathea, Antipatris, and maybe even Samaria again, before finally arriving at Caesarea on the coast of the 'Great Sea'. Here we have another aspect of Philip's evangelistic method: itinerancy.

When Philip was first sent to Samaria under the divine providence of God, it seems his plan was not to move around the area, but to stay in the city, as God was clearly working in those Samaritans in a powerful way. Yet God then sent him to speak to a particular key person—the Ethiopian eunuch—after which Philip was once again on the move. It seems that he did not choose another city close by and set up an evangelistic work there, in the hope of replicating the work at Samaria. Rather, we read that he travelled, not only to preach the gospel, but to do so as a travelling evangelist in the main cities beyond Jerusalem, until he felt the guiding hand of God cause him to settle in the city of Caesarea. What was Philip doing on his visits to these other cities? Surely God could simply have called him to travel to Caesarea without stopping off at all these cities in between?

In the work of evangelism I have learned a few lessons. One of those lessons is that not only are there evangelistic seasons, but also there are evangelistic places.

First, there evangelistic *seasons*. I have now been a full-time evangelist for over twelve years, working within the context of the British Army. Before that, I was involved in evangelistic outreaches, missions and other gospel initiatives pretty much ever since I became a Christian, almost thirty years ago. During the last twelve years there have been seasons of incredible blessing: when people have become Christians, doors have been flung wide open, and there has been perpetual joy in the work of evangelism. However, there have been other times when the work has simply been seed-sowing without very much, if any, reaping: when doors have seemed firmly closed, and when being an evangelist has been a difficult calling.

There are various possible explanations for these seasons. One factor could be the partners we have in gospel work. I remember seasons of great blessing in the work as times when God allowed us to join shoulders with others, not only as gospel workers, but also as close Christian friends. It seems that in such times, the real blessing seemed to be an outworking of a joint mission to our locality. Another factor could be the issue of leadership. As a Scripture Reader with SASRA, I work under the leadership of chaplains within the British Army. I have noticed that, when a chaplain is posted to the place where I am working, if that chaplain is mission-minded and keen to see the work of the gospel advance, then a season of blessing usually ensues. If a chaplain is more concerned about pastoral issues or counselling, or for whatever reason does not have mission as a priority, then the work of gospel ministry normally slows down. My work rate, passion and zeal do not slow down, but Christian leadership has a definite disproportionate impact on a locality, such that, when mission is a priority with the leadership, blessing in mission generally follows. When mission is further down the priority list, there is some kind of spiritual dynamic which plays out in a slowing of gospel impact. So there are clear seasons within the work of evangelistic ministry.

Second, there are also evangelistic *places* in the work of the gospel. In Matthew 10:5–15 Jesus called the disciples to be labourers in the harvest which he had spoken about in Matthew 9:37–38. He gave them certain specific instructions, such as preaching, performing miracles, what to take on their journey, and so on. He also told them,

Chapter 7

Now whatever city or town you enter, inquire who in it is worthy, and stay there till you go out. And when you go into a household, greet it. If the household is worthy, let your peace come upon it. But if it is not worthy, let your peace return to you. And whoever will not receive you nor hear your words, when you depart from that house or city, shake off the dust from your feet. Assuredly, I say to you, it will be more tolerable for the land of Sodom and Gomorrah in the day of judgment than for that city! (10:11–15).

Jesus is clearly telling the disciples that, after they have begun to preach, they will need to discern whether there is receptivity to the gospel message or not. If the people in a particular place are receptive, then the disciples should stay and continue the work of evangelism; but if they are not receptive, the disciples should leave and move on to another place, in the hope that they will eventually arrive at a place of effective gospel work. Was this the model Philip was employing in his itinerant ministry, as he travelled from Azotus to Caesarea? It looks as if this might have been a direct outworking of the evangelistic method which Jesus taught his disciples.

So Philip left Azotus, travelled north to Caesarea, and preached the gospel in all of the major cities on the way. Truly this man was an evangelist! Having arrived at Caesarea, he must have found a place of receptivity and further opportunity, for it was in this great and heavily populated trade city that Philip eventually settled and established an evangelistic ministry. If the evangelist's desire is to win souls, it makes perfect sense to be established in a place that has a great number of them. We know that Philip stayed here, because we meet him again in the city in Acts 21:8–9 (the first time we find Philip being called an 'evangelist' in Scripture), along with his four daughters, who all had the spiritual gift of prophecy. Clearly, the family was a godly one. Historians have worked out that approximately twenty years had passed between Philip's arrival in Caesarea and this cameo appearance in Acts 21:8–9. We can therefore conclude that his evangelistic work was not only continuing in Caesarea, but actually blossoming to some degree; otherwise, would Philip have remained there so long?

From this account we can see that, as well as the providential scattering, resulting in the revival at Samaria, being sent to the Ethiopian eunuch on the desert road to Gaza, and carrying out the itinerant evangelistic preaching between Azotus and Caesarea, there was also a place for a more settled work in Philip's calling in Caesarea—and so it is in evangelistic ministry today.

I am inspired by many evangelists spanning the history of the church: Philip, Patrick, John Wesley, George Whitefield, William Booth, Billy Sunday, W. P. Nicholson, to name a few. But one perhaps unheralded evangelist who inspires me in my current work is Frank Jenner. Frank was a sailor in the mid-twentieth century who was converted after trying to teach a group of Christians how to play cards. Following his conversion, he felt so overwhelmingly grateful for what Jesus Christ had done for him on the cross, and for calling him to salvation, that he wanted to demonstrate his own love for his Saviour through some kind of Christian service. He did not necessarily feel the call to be an ordained minister, but he eventually felt led to carry out some evangelistic work around George Street, at Sydney Harbour, Australia, which is where he and his family eventually settled. This would be Frank Jenner's 'Caesarea'.

His evangelistic method revolved around asking one question: 'If you were to die tonight, where would you spend eternity—in heaven or in hell?' Alongside asking this question, Frank would distribute gospel tracts which explained the message of salvation. With a pleasant manner and a stout heart, Frank went out each day to George Street with the intention of asking at least ten people that very challenging question. This was his evangelistic service for his Master. It is estimated that, over many years, Frank Jenner asked that question to approximately 100,000

Chapter 7

people! He became known as the George Street Evangelist, and he lived his life to see others hear the message by which he had been saved.

In an incredible twist to the story, English Bible teacher Francis Dixon heard of the George Street Evangelist and talk of him on his many travels around the world. To his amazement, when he visited churches and told the story of Frank Jenner in many countries and in many different kinds of churches, often someone would come up to him after the meeting and say something like this: 'I am one of those who was asked that question. I could not get it out of my mind for weeks, until eventually I went to a church and now I have become a born-again Christian!' This type of testimony was replicated all over the world. Francis Dixon was so moved by these testimonies that he decided to visit this evangelist in Australia for himself and relay these stories of conversion back to Frank Jenner. Frank was moved to tears; he revealed that he had heard of very few people responding with a definite commitment to his searching question. However, he just sensed that he needed to share this great news of salvation with as many people as he could, as a sign to Jesus of his gratitude for what he had done for him on the cross. Francis Dixon was wonderfully able to encourage Frank Jenner in his gospel work. And what a work! As an evangelist myself, I find great comfort in the Frank Jenner story: that of a man committed to the gospel, committed to people, but ultimately committed to his Lord.

Philip was scattered, sent and finally settled in the great gospel adventures which Jesus his Lord had for him. What an honour is the calling to be a witness for Jesus Christ! Whether that witness is borne out of providential guidance, through specific direction from God, through simply having the desire to spread the message of the cross to as many people as possible, or even in a settled, systematic and strategic manner—it is an honour to be a herald for God in this challenging generation.

Perhaps, like me, you are not finding yourself moving from town to town and city to city preaching the gospel in great city-wide campaigns.

Itinerant and static

Maybe your situation is more of the settled kind. We can still take encouragement and lessons from the life of Philip: that even though he had experience in city-wide revival, had divinely inspired, specific guidance to speak to an important official, and had an exciting itinerant ministry moving from city to city, his longevity in evangelistic work centred around one location—being settled in Caesarea. This means that he somehow carved out a ministry for the gospel that was not as such already established there, and he maintained it for perhaps over twenty years. We often see evangelists simply as stadium or tent preachers who move around and wow the crowds with their oratory and dynamic abilities. But if there is one thing we grasp from Philip's role as an evangelist, it is that he was simply a messenger empowered by the Spirit of God and determined to preach Jesus wherever he went, whether on his journeys or static in the city of Caesarea. He was called to be an evangelist, and an evangelist he was.

I challenge you to consider the work of evangelism. Philip was clearly an appointed and anointed man, seeing revival, infiltrating cities and establishing an important witness in the great city of Caesarea. But look at Frank Jenner: static in his home city, undramatic in his approach, not seeing revival or even much fruit, but committed to disseminating the greatest story ever told in a very simple way. You may not necessarily be called to be an evangelist, but we are all called to be witnesses for Jesus Christ. Is there some way you could be involved, right where you are—in your work, in your family, among your circle of friends, in your church, or even on the street—in sharing the message of a Saviour who died for sinners the world over in order to set them free from sin, death and hell? No, it is not easy; at times it is even fairly frightening; but it is the most glorious work I know, and, whether the world recognizes it or not, this work carries a mantle of honour with it. Why don't you pray that God would use you in gospel work right where you are. Who knows where those initial few steps might take you!

Conclusion

This insight into the life of Philip has hopefully been not only informative, but inspirational. The man who used to serve widows in the local church in Jerusalem went on to lead a revival in Samaria, left the revival for the sake of one lost soul on a journey to Ethiopia, travelled from city to city preaching the gospel, and eventually settled in the busy harbour town of Caesarea. His evangelistic passion alone is enough to challenge even the most active of Christians!

To close, let us simply draw some well-needed applications from Philip's life, ministry, drive and focus.

First, I suggest that Philip was a prepared servant before he was ever a revival evangelist. I believe in the setting apart of men and women to be used by God as fundamentally being the choosing of God over and above personal desires or church committees. Philip was chosen as a vessel prepared for service. Yet this preparation came not in preaching to the masses or in establishing a well-known city church; it came in the daily tending to disgruntled widows. When God chooses his servants, he also prepares them in the best possible way, whether that be in behind-the-scenes service or through testing, pressure and even calamity that stiffens the spine for future use. When God calls, he equips, yes—but he often does it in a way which causes us to ask questions about the path of preparation he chooses for us. For the potential revival evangelist Philip, that path was quietly to serve the needs of vocally unhappy widows.

When God does eventually launch us into our life's mission, it may not be by means of an audible voice in the middle of the night or by an angelic visitor on our doorstep! Philip was providentially sent to Samaria on the back of a very heated time of persecution. It may have seemed at the time as if God was not in full control of the situation, but he most certainly

Conclusion

was. Regarding my own calling to the evangelistic work I am currently employed in, I did not initially consider it to be a viability. Expecting nothing more than a welcome and a cup of tea, I went to speak to Jim Moore, Area Representative for Northern Ireland for the work of SASRA, simply in order to appease another Christian soldier who had suggested more than once that I would do well in this work. As Jim spoke about evangelism to soldiers, I could clearly sense the calling of God. It was completely unexpected! A divine providence led me there, not just a chance meeting. Likewise, Philip was providentially sent to Samaria, and how God vindicated that sending! Perhaps as well as asking God to use us in his service, we should also trust that he is always guiding, leading and presenting opportunities to us providentially in our daily lives, and we should learn to take those opportunities to serve him, whether in a revival or simply by speaking to an individual.

Philip's clear message was Jesus. He was not a pet-doctrine evangelist. This biblical model of the evangelist was committed to preaching the person of Jesus Christ: that he is the Son of God who was sent to rescue a sin-sick world from sin and who offers an imputed righteousness based on the work at Calvary and on nothing else; that he died, was buried and rose again, according to the Scriptures, and will return one day to judge the living and the dead. This was the message of Philip the evangelist. In our day, when the cultural cry of our generation is that we must entertain, grab the attention or just impress, let us be resolved that if we are to preach the gospel, we are to preach the gospel as it is revealed in Scripture. Social action may have its place in evangelistic practice, but it is only ever to be pre-evangelism; it is not evangelism itself. Our message is not about projects but about a person.

If we are to be preachers of the gospel, we should expect a spiritual backlash. The interface between the saved and the unsaved—the Christian and the lost—is normally found along battle lines for the human soul. In such a context, apologetics has its place, as we are

Conclusion

certainly to engage the mind in evangelism. Academic approaches may also help, as we are to be wise as serpents in our dealings with the world. However, we should always remember that the anointing of God on his written Word is the greatest weapon we can use. The 'sword of the Spirit' is what we need to wield in evangelism, not our charisma, funny jokes or clever anecdotes. These additions may help, but they must serve only as props for the real truth of Scripture. Whatever backlash we receive from the powers of darkness, the Word of God under the unction of the Spirit of God is well able to counteract it.

When it comes to the role of the Holy Spirit in the life of the born-again believer, I do not offer any opinion on how to understand this great third person of the Trinity. However, the clear biblical mandate of those involved in the early church was to covet the empowering of the Holy Spirit in order to be effective in their witness to Jesus Christ. Wherever you stand regarding the place of the Holy Spirit in the Christian life, it is surely clear that if we are truly filled with the Holy Spirit of the living God, not only will our own lives be the better for it, but also the world around us will benefit from bold, passionate and biblical warriors for Christ at a time when gospel certainty is the great need.

Finally, having seen Philip's obedience in leaving Samaria, going to the desert road and sharing with the Ethiopian eunuch, preaching the gospel from city to city, and settling in Caesarea, we are left with the undoubtedly challenging lifestyle of a man who put his Saviour before his safety, his God before his wishes, and his calling before his pleasure. What a man Philip was! And yet he was simply a Christian who had the will to serve, and to see where that simplicity of a heart for service allowed him to be taken by a God who delights in using his servants beyond their own abilities and into the greatest of gospel adventures. I personally thank God for the eighth chapter of Acts!

But where does all of this leave us? As I watch the news reports and engage with people around me on a daily basis, I see that people are

Conclusion

searching for hope. While radical Islam tries to dominate the planet, political correctness is trying to silence the church, and broken society is trying to normalize lifestyles which fifty years ago would never have been tolerated, this world is in dire need of hope. Money will never deliver it, politics can never achieve it, movies can only suggest it, and sinful pleasure can only temporarily grant a shadow of it. The only hope for this world is in receiving the saving grace of its Creator, Jesus Christ. That is the only answer for this dying old world. And right at the centre of this process is the church: global and local. We are the bearers of this great salvation message, and also examples of its power to save and to keep. God is calling us back to the place where we stop playing games with his mandate and are re-filled with his Spirit, in order to go out once again, with the name of Jesus Christ on our lips, into a world lost in sin, and to capture it for the glory of God. We may not be hailed as heroes or paraded as celebrities for doing so, but there will be rejoicing in heaven for even one lost soul who commits his or her life to Jesus Christ as a result of you and I having said, 'Yes, I will go.' And alongside the cloud of witnesses who have left us the legacy of a gospel-preaching example—such as Patrick, Whitefield, Sunday and Booth—encouraging us to march on will be the voice of our Saviour himself, urging, pleading, calling and commanding us to 'Go into all the world and preach the gospel to every creature' (Mark 16:15)!